THE **ROAD** TO **EXCELLENCE**

THE **ROAD** TO **EXCELLENCE**

6 LEADERSHIP STRATEGIES
to Build a Bulletproof Business

DAVID MATTSON
President/CEO, Sandler Training

Hardcover: 978-0-692-05386-7

E-book: 978-0-692-05387-4

This is dedicated to the entrepreneurs—the ones who do so much more than their fair share of all the working, worrying, winning, losing, and growing. You are, to quote the poet Arthur O'Shaughnessy, the "music makers, ...the dreamers of dreams, ...the movers and shakers of the world forever, it seems."

CONTENTS

Part Two: The Excellence Process

Acknowledgments

My deep thanks go to Bill Matthews for his insightful ideas based on his life's passion and for his ongoing support of this project.

I'd also like to acknowledge the thousands of entrepreneurial clients whom we have had the honor of serving over the years. It was their trust in us, and in the work of our founder David Sandler, that made this book possible. I would be remiss if I failed to note the contributions of the trainers around the world who represent Sandler, many of whom contributed ideas that ended up here.

In addition, I must thank Yusuf Toropov, who took my words and concepts and breathed life into them to create a book of which we are all very proud. My deep gratitude also goes out to John Armstrong, Margaret Stevens Jacks, Rachel Miller, Michael Norton, Steve Howell, Jennifer Willard, Laura Matthews, Jerry Dorris, Lori Ames, Frank Cespedes, Dave Hiatt, Daryl Burgess, Holly Rhoads, Mike Montague, Jeff Nay, and Désirée Pilachowski for their many and varied contributions to this project.

company into the top tier, where it belongs. Here's the difficult part: Your answer to that question is going to take a little time to uncover.

What Is Excellence?

You might wonder what I mean by "excellence." I'm using the word to refer to a business that is so impeccably managed in every aspect of its operation that no matter how closely you scrutinize its daily practices, you can't find any area where it needs help. Or, if something isn't exactly what it should be, the leader is already aware of it and is taking the necessary steps to correct it.

In addition, this business is growing and expanding, moving appropriately beyond its comfort zone to adjust to changing market conditions and technologies. When there are surprises, as there inevitably are, those surprises don't threaten the existence of the business.

Last but certainly not least, continuous improvement is a way of life at these companies. There is a circular, recurring planning

---

Words of Excellence to Live By

"The happy life is thought to be one of excellence. Now, an excellent life requires exertion. It does not consist in amusement."

—ARISTOTLE

process that pursues quality for its own sake. The leaders go through the entire organization on a regular basis, department by department, looking at each objectively, identifying what's working along with what's not working as well as it could. When they are done with this company-wide reality check, they start all over again. (By the way, their team leaders do the same thing, making sure that their specific area is constantly being improved.)

That's this book's definition of an excellent business—and they're few and far between.

So two big questions are:

1. How close are you to that excellent standard right now, and what obstacles stand in the way? (We'll look at some possible answers in Chapters 1 through 15, which are focused on what I call the "blind-spots syndrome.")

2. What is your best way forward in overcoming those obstacles? (We'll be looking at the best responses to that question in Chapters 16 through 22, by focusing on a powerful, proven management process called the Six P's.)

In considering these two big questions, we've found it helpful to classify businesses into four general categories:

→ **Excellent.** Here, professional management is a daily reality, exemplified by a disciplined, sequential, continuous, and repeatable process that propels the business into the upper 5% of organizations. These companies are always improving their present situation—and always looking forward. For leaders, and everyone else at these organizations, excellence is a way of life.

→ **Well-Managed.** Well-managed, respected in their industry, and likely in the top 25% of businesses measured in terms of professional management, these organizations are nevertheless vulnerable, because they have not yet created a management culture in which organizational excellence is second nature, regardless of personnel changes.

→ **Average.** These businesses are doing well enough to reasonably satisfy the owners and management, but they are vulnerable to regressing back to the at-risk level (see below).

→ **At-Risk.** Business owners/leaders in this group have lost control of their companies and possibly their personal lives.

Leadership and Blind Spots

I'd like to draw your attention to something important about the at-risk category. These businesses typically revolve around their leader.

Insight of Excellence

Businesses that rely primarily on one person for all or most of the decisions have low growth potential—and are likely to enter and remain in the at-risk category.

If something were to happen to these leaders, something that took them out of action for a quarter or more, the businesses would instantly be in crisis and might not survive at all. By the same token, if a group leader were to leave the company, the department might suffer greatly. One or two charismatic individuals end up carrying a disproportionate share of responsibility for the organization's performance. The stories of organizations who consistently operate in this category generally don't end well in the long term. They all have a downward trajectory that's caused by the blind-spots syndrome: They don't know what they don't know about the obstacles they face, and they're not interested in finding out. This dysfunctional way of working drains both leaders and organizations of energy, resilience, and potential.

As it happens, there are certain predictable ways that a blind-spots syndrome develops. At Sandler, the global training and consulting organization I am privileged to lead, we've noticed that the businesses in the at-risk and well-managed categories typically fall prey to more than half of these common management issues. This is troubling because even one of these blind spots has the potential to undermine or even kill a business.

In fact, the odds are good that you and your organization have more than one blind spot to address right now. It's essential that you learn to recognize each of these blind spots as a flashing red-light warning—a sign of trouble on the horizon. These are the roadblocks that stand in the path to excellence. If left unattended, they invariably lead to organizational underperformance, stress, or even burnout. All the blind spots are important enough to learn about and recognize. They can pop up when you least

Words of Excellence to Live By

"If there's more than one way to do a job and one of those ways will end in disaster, then somebody will do it that way."

—An early formulation of Murphy's Law, published in *People* magazine, 1983; attributed to **EDWARD A. MURPHY**

expect them, even in the areas where you imagine yourself and your company to be the least vulnerable.

Companies often fall into a trap: They "fix" a blind spot, but for some mysterious reason find that it returns over time. Here's why that happens. Creating self-sufficient team members and departments is the ultimate goal of any effective leader. That means people and teams make important decisions in areas you've specifically delegated to them—which is as it should be. As you grow in scale or bring in new people, that very growth creates the possibility of a blind spot's recurrence or of brand new blind spots developing—new problem areas of which you and other company leaders aren't aware. The fact that there were no blind spots in a given area the last time you checked is no guarantee that there are no blind spots right now. Traveling the road to excellence means assuming that there are going to be bumps and potholes along the way.

Achieving Excellence

In Part Two of this book, you'll learn about the six powerful leadership strategies that can make excellence a daily reality in your organization. We call them the Six P's. I don't want to share a lot about these six steps with you first because I've found that this proven system for organizational excellence tends to make the most sense and to be followed most consistently once leaders have had the chance to identify the blind spots they've been living with in their businesses—sometimes for years or decades. Recognizing these blind spots is usually a sobering experience, one that tends to motivate people to take action.

Suffice to say that Part One of the book is meant to make you a believer in the importance of implementing what you'll be reading in Part Two. Taken together, the two halves are designed, not just to give you theoretical insights, but to make achieving excellence a way of doing business and a way of life.

Let's get started!

PART ONE

The Blind-Spots Syndrome

The blind spots you'll be reading about in Part One of this book can adversely affect you or any leader within your organization, regardless of your industry or the size of your company. They're easy to miss—and they're capable of causing immense damage without ever being noticed. I call the act of ignoring or minimizing these issues the blind-spots syndrome. We'll look at the most common blind spots in the chapters that follow.

1

Blind Spot: Not Being in Recruiting Mode

Are you looking, right now, for the talent that your company will need for the next phase of its growth?

When was the last time you or someone on your team interviewed a candidate, even though there wasn't a formal opening in your company?

Are there any key people who might leave your organization over the next six to twelve months whom you would find difficult or impossible to replace?

How strong is your bench?

Talent is the ultimate resource. The very best companies are always on the lookout for the best people. They are always building the bench. Like a professional sports team, your organization should always be looking for talent, both internal and external—and growing that talent.

It's very common for company leaders to watch parts of their organizations spiral into crisis when a (supposedly) "irreplaceable" individual departs unexpectedly, leaving gaping knowledge and skill holes, damaging customer relationships, or causing major delays to key projects. This is one area where you really do need to take Murphy's Law into account—the one that emphasizes your responsibility, as a leader, to expect that everything that can go wrong will go wrong. Even though you may not want to, you have to assume that the people you need most are the ones who can be expected to leave at the worst possible times.

Another dangerous aspect of this blind spot is the all-too-common failure to recruit with an eye to the future. It's not enough to ask who you need on staff to do what needs doing today. You need to ask who you need to do what you will need to do. You should be recruiting for future roles. Your company's needs are constantly changing, the market is constantly changing, and the organization is constantly changing. The people you need today from a talent perspective may not be the people that you need next year or five years from now. Based on a sound multi-year plan, you should start recruiting based on the talent that you're going to need in order to achieve your future goals.

I was working with a CEO recently who found herself paying dearly for this very blind spot. A vice president on whom the CEO over-relied for a great deal was offered a bigger, more attractive job at another firm. She left with only minimal notice—during a major rollout of a new technology platform. There was no one to take this executive's place. This one personnel change set the company back almost a year and cost the organization hundreds

Words of Excellence to Live By

"Whether your company produces cars or cosmetics, hiring great people for a business is always the most important task. After all, a company is only as good as the people it keeps."

—JIM COLLINS

of thousands of dollars. No, this kind of thing doesn't happen every day. But if it happens to you once, that's too many times.

Ask yourself, "What would happen if these key people left? Who would take their place?" If you don't have a good answer, then you need to focus on building up your bench. At our company I constantly ask myself, "If so-and-so left, who would replace that person?" If I don't have an answer, then I start looking. Can you imagine a professional sports team not working without a comprehensive depth chart that went at least two or three people deep for each position? Neither can I. The reason sports teams operate this way is that management knows that unforeseen events like injuries can happen at any moment. Not preparing for such a situation could put the team in deep trouble—or even destroy a whole season's worth of work. The same basic dynamic applies in business.

This does not necessarily mean that you have to invest huge amounts of your own personal time in the recruiting function, nor does it mean you personally have to hire all the people in your organization. What fixing this blind spot does mean, though, is that as you meet new people or hear about new people, you should be thinking about how they might fit into your short- and long-term recruitment plans. Whenever I meet someone new, I ask myself, "Would that person be good here? What would that person be able to do for the company?" I always find good people, and even though I might not always have a spot for them at that moment, I make a point of keeping in touch. Six months or so down the line, when there's an opening, I reach out. We've made a lot of great hires that way.

When it comes to recruiting, it's important to think in the long term—not just about the jobs you've got open right now, but also the jobs you will need to fill in order to sustain your next stage of growth. At our company, for instance, we looked forward and realized the way we serviced our customer was changing. This meant we were going to have to change as an organization and that meant we needed to adjust our recruiting strategy. We started paying attention to the human resource needs we were going to have, in roles that didn't yet exist. Once we knew what we would be doing 12, 24, and 36 months down the line, we could start thinking proactively about who would be filling those roles.

Here's an example of what I mean. We have an engineering company as a client. Its engineers, like most professional service providers, are expected to go through continuous education programs and earn professional development credits in order to keep their designations. One of the company's senior managers was attending one of those required classes. He was expecting it to be a long day, and he didn't expect to get much from the session. He was really hoping only to pick up a few insights, check his emails, talk to a few of his team members on the breaks, and get to the end of the day. But lo and behold, there was a woman sitting across the table from him asking the program instructor good questions at every opportunity.

The questions this woman was asking piqued the curiosity and the interest of the senior manager. The two of them struck up a conversation over lunch; the manager asked her to stay in touch. Long story short: That manager wasn't looking for a new employee on the morning of that continuing education program, but he was thinking about his company's long-term priorities. That's why, four months later, the woman had a new job at my client company. This new hire has since made major contributions totaling millions of dollars. That would have never happened if the manager hadn't been in "always be recruiting" mode.

It's always good to have a list of three or four people you could approach for any given role you may need to fill. Being in constant recruiting mode also gives you the flexibility to disqualify an applicant who isn't right for the job. You never know who's going to say "yes" and who's going to say "no." You want to leave yourself plenty of options.

TAKEAWAY QUESTIONS

→ What do you currently do when you receive an inbound resume or referral for someone who could add value to your organization and you do not have an opening?

→ Who are the people you would really like to work with one day—the people who could add the most value to your organization?

→ What critical roles on your team would you have the most difficulty filling if someone left unexpectedly?

2

Blind Spot: Not Establishing a Process for Hiring

How do you avoid bad hires?

What three or four steps do you consistently follow to find the best possible applicant?

How do you counteract the "halo effect"—the tendency to hold a bias in favor of an applicant's superficial qualities that may remind you of past successful applicants (or even yourself)?

You already know that a "gut feeling" is not enough when it comes to making a hire. Now it's time to take action on what you know. You need a clear, quantifiable hiring process, and everyone who hires employees needs to understand it and be able to follow it.

Creating and refining this process is one of the core responsibilities of a leader. You've got to bring the right types of people into your organization in order to reach your goals. When there's no process in place for doing that, you place your organization at risk.

This is because a bad hire has ripple effects within the organization; you end up hiring people who either don't have the skills and experience to get the job done or have a bad attitude.

Bad hires are extremely expensive. A bad sales hire, for instance, will typically cost you five times the amount of salary over just the first 18 months. (Each company has its own unique number, but I am willing to bet the number you are actually working with will take your breath away, like my estimate just did.) This takes into consideration all the time and energy that it takes for you to interview the bad hires, get them up to speed, and create and maintain all the necessary support systems. That's a big investment, and it's one you'll only want to make with great care.

Understand: Your job in the hiring process is to disqualify the candidates who will not excel at your company. So often, as a leader, you want to fill an open position as quickly as possible. You may tend to look at pressing project issues. You may not spot the larger, more important question: whether you have a process

Insight of Excellence

Identify the cost of a single bad hire for your organization, including all the time invested in recruitment, training, support, benefits, taxes, and so on. The cost, assuming an 18-month stay, is likely to be something on the order of five times the person's annual salary.

in place that would help you identify if this person truly would be successful at your firm.

Have you thought about what the role does? Have you identified all the characteristics and skills necessary to succeed in this position? Do you interview and hire in a way that reflects the realities of the job to confirm the presence of all the qualities necessary to perform it well? When you don't have a process, it's easy to imagine you're doing these things when you really aren't.

Recently, I was working with an organization whose inside salespeople never actually met with prospects and customers face-to-face. The salespeople did their job exclusively on the phone. Yet the hiring interviews were entirely conducted in person. Shouldn't a fair amount of those interviews have been conducted on the phone? Of course you want to meet the people in person, but if 100% of the job requires the person to establish rapport over the phone, lead the call, and set a next step, you'll probably want to hear how well the applicant does all that when you call his cell number. Put those applicants in that situation as you interview and hire them. That should be part of your process.

One non-negotiable part of my hiring process when I'm considering people for a key executive position is to go to dinner with the candidates and their spouse/significant other. You would be amazed at the insights you can pick up over a meal. For instance, if the position we're hiring for involves heavy travel, I can ask the spouse, "Just out of curiosity, how do you feel about your spouse traveling 60% of the time?" If the answer comes back, "Yeah, that's been the way it is for years; it's not an issue," no problem. But if the person pauses for a moment, looks uncomfortable, and says,

"Well, wait a minute, that's an awful lot of time on the road," then you know that there's not going to be harmony in the household on this issue, and that's something you need to take into account.

When you have a process for hiring, you know exactly what you're going to do ahead of time and during the interview process itself. You know what the job profile is and what the perfect candidate looks like. You know what questions you plan to ask in order to understand whether the person fits the job, and you can target those questions so that they're focused broadly on big-picture issues in the early stages of the process and more closely on specific experience and insights in the later stages. As the interview process moves forward, you're going to learn more about people; you're going to discover how they think and how they would react in specific situations that are common in your workplace.

Because it's a process, it's documented. That means that other people—not just you—can follow the same steps and avoid the same common problems that lead to bad hires (such as making a hiring decision based on a superficial, and ultimately meaningless, resemblance to a past top performer). When you've got a good hiring process, you know exactly what skills and aptitudes you're looking for and you don't get misled by superficial factors. You've also got built-in safeguards for particularly important positions, such as aptitude assessments and interviews involving multiple people from your side. That's what a good hiring process looks like. Most organizations don't have such a process—and that means they operate at a major competitive disadvantage to companies that do.

TAKEAWAY QUESTIONS

→ Good or bad, what was the result of the last two hires you made when the decision was based on "gut feel," rather than on following a hiring process?

→ What is the hiring process you currently follow?

→ If you do not have a hiring process, what are the criteria you believe should be included in an effective hiring process for your organization?

3

Blind Spot: Not Tying Personal Goals to Corporate Goals

Can you name the most important personal goals (not business goals) of the people who report to you?

Can each of your senior managers name the most important personal goals (not business or financial goals) of the people who report to them?

Sometimes, leaders fall into the trap of believing that people are going to work harder for their employer than they will for their families or their own futures. This is simply not true. Human beings always have been and always will be driven to improve their own personal situation. You must tap into that motivation.

You set your corporate goals, you get excited about those goals, and you believe that because you pay people's salaries and they are dedicated, professional employees that they're going to get excited, too. You assume that that they'll put in 1,000% each and every day, 24/7, just like you do. And then you're surprised when that doesn't happen.

Of course, you do have to identify corporate goals clearly, set the key performance indicators, and figure out how compensation fits in. All that's essential. But you also have to take into account the reality that people will always work a whole lot harder for themselves and their families than they will ever work for you. That's not any reflection on the employee. That's human nature.

Think about it. I'm your employee. What scenario am I most likely to take action on?

→ Scenario A: You tell me I could earn a $10,000 bonus as part of doing my job well.

→ Scenario B: I realize I have to find a way to save $10,000 in order to send my child to college, or I want to take a $10,000 company-paid vacation to some destination I've always wanted to visit.

I will always come up with faster and more efficient ways to take care of business in Scenario B. Once I'm engaged on a personal level, there's a powerful driving force that takes over. Your job as the leader isn't to repeat the corporate performance goal to me. It's to help me connect the dots, to link that corporate performance goal to my personal goal.

As a leader, you know that, day after day, your people are faced with doing things that are possibly uncomfortable for them. You want to make sure that they're motivated to get done what needs to be done. You want to make sure that they're not stuck in their comfort zones. You also know that it's very common for people to

Words of Excellence to Live By

"All who have accomplished great things have had a great aim, have fixed their gaze on a goal which was high, one which sometimes seemed impossible."

—ORISON SWETT MARDEN

reach a plateau, a place where they're comfortable, a place they're not really learning and growing very much and they're not asking themselves the tough questions. Guess what? When people are comfortable, they work at about 60–70% of their capacity. If you don't connect the dots for them, that's where they stay: In that 60–70% zone.

You want your people to have the best possible perspective about how to invest the hours in their day. As a leader, you know that if it's a Friday afternoon and it's sunny out, even though golf or tennis or something else you love to do during your leisure time might look good that day, that doesn't necessarily mean those options are the best possible use of your time. You want to make it easy for your people to reach the same conclusion, but based on their own goals. If they're only tied into a corporate goal that's coming to them from a third party, they may accept that goal at an intellectual level, but there's not going to be much emotional attachment to that goal. (Some team members may buy into the corporate goal on an emotional level because they have strong internal competitive drive, but you can't count on that for everyone.)

To avoid the stressful situation where you are the only person who's emotionally invested in attaining the corporate goal, we strongly suggest that you learn to tie corporate goals to personal goals. Let's take the example of Juanita, a salesperson who is working on commission. Let's say Juanita's annual quota is $1 million dollars, and her commission on this would be $100,000. You could simply sit Juanita down and say, "Here are the numbers: your quota is a million dollars, and your commission rate is 10%. You've got a great territory. Go for it." What's going to happen? Chances are that there would be pushback at some level. If you are lucky, you'd hear about that pushback during the meeting and perhaps be able to deal with it. But if you aren't lucky (and who is, all the time?), you'd end the meeting thinking you'd accomplished something, Juanita would smile politely as she left, and you'd have no idea that she was spending every coffee break complaining to her coworkers about how unfair it is that she has absolutely no input about her annual sales targets.

But suppose that meeting went a little differently. Suppose you said, "Look, if you make your goal, Juanita, you're going to receive $100,000. Let's pretend for a second that you achieved that goal. What would you do with your $100,000?" Suppose you let Juanita think about that possibility and process it on her own. What would she come up with?

She might say something like this: "Well, I would put money toward retirement. I might put a down payment on a vacation home for my family, and I'd be able put some of the money away for college for my daughter; she's only eleven, but I know she's going to need a good education." Now you can have a better discussion!

Knowing what Juanita's goals are, you know what to manage to when you're talking to her over the course of the year. You can meet with her on a quarterly basis and talk about her goals—which happen to be your goals, too. If you find a way to remind her about her vacation home, about her retirement plans, about saving for her daughter's college fund, that's going to be far more motivating to Juanita than another lecture about the importance of hitting quota. If you do that, you'll find that Juanita will work harder. She'll be much more aggressive and focused in trying to achieve her goal, because now it connects to something personal.

I've given you a sales example, but the basic principle I'm talking about connects to every single manager/employee relationship in your organization. This powerful connect-the-dots discussion (which saves you immense amounts of time later on) really does need to happen. Your managers must gain a deep understanding of the personal aspirations of all those who report to them. That means you must lead the way by gaining a clear understanding of the personal aspirations of all of your direct reports.

TAKEAWAY QUESTIONS

→ What are the top three corporate goals and objectives of your organization?

→ If you were going to share your most important corporate goals with your direct reports, what would that sound like?

→ What are the top personal goals of your direct reports?

4

Blind Spot: Not Building a Culture of Accountability

Do you set clear expectations that can't be misunderstood?

Do your people take personal responsibility ... or blame others for mistakes and failures?

Do your people know exactly what is required on a given project, when it is required, and what the repercussions will be if there are shortfalls and delays? Have you stated those things clearly?

Do you notice and acknowledge when you don't follow through on your own commitments, both large and small, to others in the organization?

Many business leaders talk about operating within a culture of accountability—but then turn around and unknowingly sabotage that culture in their interactions with their own direct reports. All too often, this leads to a dysfunctional team culture rooted in finger-pointing and missed deadlines. Leaders at these organizations miss the point. Accountability is mostly about living up to your own commitments and creating an environment where others do that, too.

Creating a culture of accountability in any organization requires that leaders at the top of the organization have the courage to show culpability when it's appropriate to do so. In other words, they model full accountability, and they openly acknowledge when they've fallen short on a particular commitment.

Our experience is that the leader's congruency is the single biggest determinant of success in this area. Without leadership from the top in the area of accountability, accountability simply does not become an important cultural value.

Here's a very simple example. Let's assume that a trait that you're aiming to instill throughout the organization is punctuality and you get stuck in traffic and show up fifteen minutes late for a meeting. You shouldn't expect to start that meeting without making reference to the fact that you were late and apologizing for that. This may seem like a small thing, but it's not. Once you take personal ownership of the choices you made that caused you to fall short in your commitments to show up on time, once you make an honest effort to let people know that a) you understand the impact of your actions and b) you want to do things differently next time, you will be making not just a personal statement, but an important cultural statement about accountability. As the saying goes, you will be walking your talk. And people will follow your example.

I learned a lot about accountability from David Sandler, the founder of our company and a man I was lucky enough to have as my trainer, coach, and mentor. Early in my career, David taught me to hold myself accountable.

Insight of Excellence

Accountability is all about doing what you say you're going to do.

He did this mostly by means of four critical leadership habits. First and foremost, he set clear goals that were measurable and he connected them to my personal aspirations. Second, he asked me a consistent set of questions about my daily and weekly behaviors during our one-on-one meetings so that these questions became predictable and I made a point of being prepared for them. Third, he set smart, measurable benchmarks and checked in on my progress at key points. For instance, if he needed something important to be complete on the first of September, he didn't start asking me about it in late August; instead, he'd ask me to discuss my progress toward that important goal on the first of each month, starting in January, so we could both see how far along I was. Fourth and perhaps most important, he walked his talk. He was congruent. His words matched his actions, and he lived by going above and beyond his commitment. When David said he was going to do something, he followed through—or if he found he couldn't, he reached out to whomever he had made his commitment to ahead of time and explained what had changed and what he thought the new expectations needed to be. This applied to big things like service commitments to clients and (seemingly) little things like showing up on time for meetings with me.

David was a truly great personal role model in the area of accountability. Because he was on time, I wanted to be on time. Because he was prepared, I wanted to be prepared. Because he followed through, I wanted to follow through. Because he acted in accordance with strong personal values, I did the same.

Creating a culture of accountability is really a matter of making accountability a consistent personal priority in your own daily life as a leader and modeling full integrity and full accountability, not only for others in your organization but for your customers and the larger world. A great example of this kind of accountability is the famous Tylenol tampering episode.

Back in the early 1980s, Tylenol and many other over-the-counter medications were sold without tamper-evident seals. In 1982, someone decided to open bottles of Tylenol, dose the capsules with cyanide, recap the bottles, and put them back on the store shelves. Seven people died. Although the lethal product sabotage only affected the Chicago area, Jim Burke, the chairman of Johnson & Johnson (the company that manufactured Tylenol), ordered a nationwide recall, halted all production and advertising, and issued warnings to hospitals and consumers to stop using Tylenol until authorities could confirm what the problem was.

Burke insisted that the company assume full accountability for handling a situation that turned out to be not its fault but was definitely its issue to resolve. Burke assumed a public role, appearing on national television to explain exactly what the company was doing to deal with the crisis and to protect people who had trusted in the quality of his product. He assumed personal responsibility for leading the company's effort to ensure public safety. He set clear expectations about his organization's commitment to share important information with the public and cooperate with law enforcement.

The recall is estimated to have cost Tylenol over $100 million, and in the short term, the product's market share collapsed. Within a few months, however, thanks to Burke's assumption of full personal and corporate accountability and the clear expectations he had set with the public, it became evident that the company was not only not at fault, but had acted responsibly and coordinated its actions with the FBI in such a way that it became a role model for other major corporations facing similar crises. Before the year was out, Tylenol was relaunched in the innovative tamper-resistant and tamper-evident packaging that is now required by the FDA for such products. Within a few years, Tylenol was once again the leading product in its category.

By assuming full accountability for the situation and by taking the rapid response steps it did—notably the step of recalling the entire nationwide inventory of Tylenol—Johnson & Johnson saved its brand. The company as a whole, and Jim Burke in particular, clearly demonstrated that taking risks with public safety was not an option and that the company could be counted on. Tylenol quickly regained the market share it had lost.

Johnson & Johnson's credo reads in part, "We believe our first responsibility is to the doctors, nurses and patients, to mothers and fathers and all others who use our products and services." To understand the vital importance of an accountable culture, one that's modeled from the top down, ask yourself these questions. What if Burke had not held himself accountable for maintaining full congruence with those words by matching them with action? What if he had stalled or stonewalled? What if he had waited for the FDA to tell him what to do? The disaster would have been a hundred times worse.

Here's the bottom line: As a leader, you can't expect accountability from others until you model it for them in person. Once you do that, amazing things can happen.

TAKEAWAY QUESTIONS

→ Does your organization currently have a culture of accountability? How do you know?

→ What does accountability mean to you personally?

→ How does your organization currently communicate expectations? How does it communicate results? Could these communications be improved? If so, how?

5

Blind Spot: Creating Learned Helplessness

Out of the last five times someone brought you a problem and asked you to fix it, how many times did you ask that person to propose a possible solution before you stepped in to solve the problem yourself?

How often do you say or think, "If I don't do this, it won't be done properly"—and then take on personal responsibility for fixing the problem?

When you are unavailable or inaccessible, does your organization stop in its tracks because people need your approval?

N o matter what industry you operate in, no matter what the size of your business is, your goal should be to develop and sustain a self-sufficient work force.

There are a number of obstacles to achieving this goal, of course. Perhaps the most obvious one is the understandable desire to save time. These days, most companies have learned to do more with less, and the tendency among many leaders is to look for ways to get to the best solution in the quickest possible way. So when an employee asks you for help, you may be tempted to just give him the answer. This seems to take less time. After all, if somebody asks, "How do I do X?" and you respond, "Just do A, B, and C," it's easy to assume that you've gotten that person "up and running" in a matter of minutes. The problem is, you haven't.

That employee has learned nothing other than the best thing to do when there's a problem is to find you and get you to solve it. Not only that, the employee assumed no accountability whatsoever for the outcome (see the previous blind spot). Think about that for a moment. In this scenario, if the solution didn't work, it's because you made a bad suggestion. But if it did work, it's because the person implemented your instructions. This is a lose/lose deal for you, the leader.

The question then becomes, not how do you get the employee to do X, but how do you make your people stronger? In other words: How do you scale yourself? You need a working environment in which people think for themselves and don't look to you for every single decision.

To combat this debilitating blind spot, effective leaders learn to ask the employee questions like:

- → "What would you have done about this if you hadn't been able to find me today?"
- → "What are your top two suggestions on how we should solve this problem?"

In many cases, your aim will be to make slight variations to the answers you hear to these kinds of questions. This not only creates a dialogue and the all-important dynamic of collaboration, but it also gives the employee ownership of, and responsibility for, the outcome in question. It's far better to edit the employee's solution than to supply one of your own.

By giving people the opportunity to think for themselves and by "unlearning" the habit of solving the problem on the spot, you can help the organization take a step towards excellence. You can reverse dysfunctional communication patterns that only undermine a sense of personal responsibility.

Words of Excellence to Live By

"In a dependent relationship, the protégé can always control the protector by threatening to collapse."

—BARBARA W. TUCHMAN

By the way, when I give talks about these blind spots before groups of leaders, it's at about this point that they start to get a little concerned. Many of them start thinking to themselves, "Wow—he's covered five blind spots, and so far we're looking at all five of them as being problems in our organization. We must be in real trouble."

Just a reminder: This first part of the book is all about shining a spotlight on the obstacles, the most common blind spots we help leaders recognize and identify. The first step, and probably the most important step, is learning to see the problem, to recognize the situation you're facing, and to accept that it is not a normal or desirable state of affairs. We'll look at the best systemic solutions to the challenges when we get into a discussion of the Six P's, a little later in the book. For now, understand that you are on the right track, and that by clearly identifying where the trouble spots are, you are gaining clarity about your own priorities as a leader and shortening your organization's eventual learning curve.

TAKEAWAY QUESTIONS

→ Think of a time when you personally jumped in to fix a problem for someone else. What was the outcome? What was the effect on team morale and effectiveness?

→ Think of a time when you allowed an employee to learn by solving a problem or handling a situation within clearly defined boundaries. What was the outcome on team morale and effectiveness?

→ What can you do to help people feel more empowered when making decisions in those areas where you have delegated authority and responsibility to them?

6

Blind Spot: Not Having a Common Organizational Language and Approach

Do your teams and work groups ever come away from meetings having heard the same words but somehow reached very different conclusions about what those words mean and do something completely different than you expected?

Do performance reviews differ throughout the company because people are using their own personal approach or definitions to describe the key activities, objectives, and completion benchmarks?

Do customers have to decode different vocabularies from different groups in your organization?

Many people, at one time or another in their lives, have had the unpleasant experience of being in a discussion where they felt like someone was speaking in a language they just didn't understand. There were all these buzz-words and insider language that they couldn't decode. As a leader, you may have had the experience of two or more people, from different parts of the organization, describe a particular common problem—but in terms that make it clear that each was in possession of a personal version of what happened and what needs to happen next. You may have also had the experience of thinking people are leaving a meeting headed in the same direction—only to learn later that they each felt entitled to head off in very different directions.

Words of Excellence to Live By

"Much unhappiness has come into the world because of bewilderment and things left unsaid."

—FYODOR DOSTOYEVSKY

These experiences are symptoms of a lack of a common language and approach. Sometimes leaders forget that it's their responsibility to make sure those kinds of disconnects happen as infrequently as possible—or, ideally, not at all. It's their responsibility to make sure that their people are using the same terminology to mean the same things and that they're communicating as effectively as possible about who's doing what, why they're doing it, and when it's needed. If leaders don't fulfill that responsibility, they run the risk of making mutual mystification part of the company culture. That's a recipe for disaster.

This blind spot can play out on two levels. The first is what I call the "macro" level: People within the same department or work group may not agree on the same way to describe key terms or critical assumptions. So for instance, I may think that a project task being complete means that I've done all that I can do on the project. But you may think that that same project task is complete when another department has signed off on all aspects of what I've done. Or, to use another example, I may consider a certain standard deliverable to a new customer as being Products A, B, and C, based on my own experience in the customer's industry. But other people who are involved with that customer may assume that the standard first order consists of Products B, C, and D, based on the orders received from customers across multiple industries. Or (and this may be the most common situation), I may use a word or phrase to describe what I'm doing that other people in my organization who are counting on me simply don't understand. For instance, if my status on a given project task is "awaiting team review," and that is supposed to mean that I need help from you to finish what I'm doing, you may not realize that I'm waiting for you to reach out to me.

At the "micro" level, the problem is that your customer-facing teams aren't on the same page. For instance, Shipping, Engineering, Sales, and Customer Support are using competing terminology to describe the same processes, issues, and products/services. In this situation, one person in your organization communicates with a customer or external stakeholder using words in a way that other people wouldn't. So your customer service team thinks "expedited shipping" means one thing—but your shipping department thinks it means something else. Here again, the potential for trouble is substantial.

This potential for conflicting or incompatible language is built into your business. It's inescapable. As a practical matter, you really can't expect this problem not to arise in some shape, form, or fashion unless you allow your people zero autonomy and zero flexibility—and that would be a huge mistake. The right response here is not to insist that everyone clear their definitions through you, but rather to encourage your people to get into the habit of identifying, with each other and with outsiders, any areas where there's going to be a possible translation problem.

You can only do that by building into the culture a value that says, "We clarify exactly what we're talking about so that there's no mutual mystification, and we confirm the real-world implications of what we're saying to each other." Failing to build this value into your culture and to reinforce it appropriately can lead to major organizational problems.

A large bank we worked with didn't have a common process for originating loans and moving them forward to completion. When employees in Florida talked about "completing the initial steps of the loan process" with a customer, they meant something very different than the employees in Chicago. This led to major problems with customers when an employee from Florida was transferred to the Chicago office and used the so-called "Florida rules" in his initial interactions with his first half-dozen or so business loan seekers. He had to re-engage with each of these people and walk them through a new set of "initial" steps, and he lost several of them along the way.

Consider too the case of the national consumer products company whose Atlanta office uses one set of processes to conduct employee performance reviews but whose San Francisco office uses an entirely different ranking and evaluation system. When it's time to hand out promotions, candidates in San Francisco who don't get the bump may become curious about why they were passed over in favor of someone from Atlanta. Wouldn't you prefer to be able to look at evaluations that used the same terminology and measured the same things? Wouldn't a common language and a common approach in the area of employee evaluations support better personnel decisions throughout the organization?

There is no one overnight solution to this problem. Solutions will present themselves as your business grows. The question is not whether you will be able to eliminate the problem entirely but whether the example that you, as leader, set for your people encourages them to identify, prioritize, and tactfully resolve possible problems with competing vocabularies and approaches. Do you reward people for doing so?

TAKEAWAY QUESTIONS

→ What are the benefits to your organization to having and following a common process?

→ If you asked others on your team to document the most important process they follow, would the answers they give for a given process match up?

→ What is one specific action you can take that will help your team create and follow a common process?

7

Blind Spot: Not Capturing Best Practices

Do you have a "playbook" your top managers use for the most important recurring activities, such as holding meetings, coaching, conducting performance reviews, or handling difficult conversations?

Do new hires have a documented, accessible summary of the best practices of the top performers in their area?

Does important "tribal knowledge" walk out the door forever when you lose a key employee?

Wouldn't it be great if the newest people in any area of your business could quickly get to the point where they seem as if they have been in the business for 25 years? Ideally, that's what documenting and sharing best practices is meant to do.

If you aren't capturing the way you want things done—by, for instance, documenting exactly what your top performers do and building their best practices into your daily management routine and your performance review processes—you are setting your organization up for failure.

Think about it. There are an awful lot of things that an individual who contributes to your organization must master. It's hard for any one individual to learn and master everything that's necessary in a short amount of time. If your goal is to make sure that your teams are self-sufficient—and as we've seen, it should be—then it's absolutely imperative that you give your people the tools and the insights they need to make them as productive as possible. You don't want them spending five years learning from the School of Hard Knocks. You want them to capitalize on other people's previous successes, those who have been doing the job at a superior level or have many years of experience that they can share and transfer to others. Answer? Create a playbook!

Of course, you have to accept that people can't be great at everything. It's impossible for everyone to become an expert, a black belt, in everything that the organization does. But you also need to recognize that, at some point, if people don't have experience or guidance as they enter a new situation, they tend to make up the best answer they can. That's a great instinct—but it's not enough. Your people want to do the right thing, but if there's no playbook for them to look to, if there's no experience that they can rely on, then they will improvise—or not do it at all. While improvising is sometimes necessary, it's not really an effective strategy on a daily basis.

Playbooks are not new. Professional sports teams have playbooks that they provide every player—players who are brand new

Words of Excellence to Live By

"If you don't have time to do it right, when will you have the time to do it over?"

—JOHN WOODEN

to the organization, but also players who are being paid tens of millions of dollars who have years and years of experience. The team gives them all the same playbook. Why? To make sure that they're all on the same page. The veterans want to make sure that they don't get stuck in a comfort zone. They use the playbook to practice and lock in what they know—and also to learn little tricks of the trade and plays that they don't execute frequently. Newcomers use the playbook to learn how to execute a certain play as if they had been in the league for years. Sports management spends immense amounts of time, effort, and energy putting together the right playbook and ensuring compliance with it. Why can't you do the same thing?

A blind spot in this area would show up in saying things like, "We have good people; they will figure it out." Or, "That's what I pay the managers for." Yes, they are great people. They will figure it out. But wouldn't it be nice if they had access to the right way to do something the very first time, in a way that you know is successful and that they can replicate as quickly as possible? Wouldn't it be nice if you didn't lose best practices forever or have to start from scratch whenever an employee decides to move to another organization?

Your job is to outline all the things someone within a job function should be able to do in order to be 100% successful. This goes for every aspect of your organization. Your job is to give people crystal-clear examples of what success looks like. If the playbook says people need to interview well, for instance, you need to give them the best known process for interviewing. You need to give them the top ten questions based on job functions they should be interviewing for to uncover whether people have the right skills, experiences, and results to succeed at this job. You need to set up a document that helps them become the best interviewer possible. You need to get it all down in black and white, not only for new managers but also for leaders who don't interview on a daily basis and who want a refresher course.

Don't make the mistake of thinking you don't have time for this. The process of creating a playbook of best practices will save you immense amounts of time in the long run. Consider, for instance, the question of how to part company with an employee who simply isn't working out. Wouldn't you want the HR person who's been with you for five years to be following the same playbook in this sensitive area as the successful HR person who's been with you for twenty years? Doesn't setting aside the minimal time to create and update such a playbook compare favorably with the amount of time necessary to address a legal challenge if a disgruntled former employee spots an inconsistency or oversight in the termination process?

Examples of areas where organizations typically need a

playbook but don't have one include (but aren't limited to): the sales process, hiring, onboarding, performance evaluations, coaching, first-line supervision, and working with partners. The to-do items here are pretty simple, and the process is straightforward. Find out who does a really good job in each of the areas that are most important to your organization, and start delegating topics. Get your seasoned veterans to participate. Make it easy for people. Have them call it in! You can record their insights, then have the discussions transcribed and edited. Once it's all down in text form, acknowledge all the contributors, celebrate their insights, and circulate the playbook to those who need it most. Don't forget to use playbooks in your onboarding process. (See the next blind spot.)

Here at Sandler we have over 600 separate pieces in our master playbook, which helps people replicate, at a high level of proficiency, each and every part of what we do. Everyone participates, and we all give high fives and compliments to those who have added new things. Adding to the playbook is part of our culture. When the competition comes out with a new product or service, we create a new page in the playbook on how to deal with that. We like ours so much we give it to our clients. Our playbook is never-ending—and yours can be, too.

It's a truly wonderful feeling when you can hand a new hire a playbook and say, "Welcome aboard. You're now part of the team. That means you get to use this playbook—the accumulated tribal knowledge of our company over the past half-century. We wrote it for you, so that you can become an expert as quickly as possible." It really engages the new hire. (See the next blind spot!)

TAKEAWAY QUESTIONS

→ On a scale of 1 to 10, with 10 being the best, how would you rate yourself and your organization when it comes to capturing and sharing best practices?

→ What two best practices can you take the lead in capturing and sharing?

→ What two best practices should others take the lead in capturing and sharing?

8

Blind Spot: Not Creating a Good Onboarding Experience

Has any of your employees ever been subjected to the "hire and forget" school of onboarding?

In evaluating the performance of new hires during their first month, have you ever said (or thought) to yourself, "They're smart; they'll figure it out"?

Do you let others in the organization onboard new hires "informally," without any documentation or process?

How long does it take a new hire to become profitable or make a contribution to your organization?

When they first come into your organization, employees desperately want to succeed. As the organization's leader, you want them to succeed, too. In all likelihood, those two objectives are never more closely aligned than they are on the person's very first day of employment. Yet what happens, time and time again? The opportunity is botched!

New employees are left to figure nearly everything out on their own, and their leaders make excuses for that decision. (Like telling themselves that they operate in a "self-starter" culture, or that they only hire seasoned veterans, or that there is no one better than their current team to deal with the onboarding process.)

Recruitment is a little like courtship. You wouldn't plan to date someone with full attentiveness, concern, care, and attention—and then suddenly stop paying attention to the person the moment you exchanged wedding vows. You know courtship is only the beginning of the journey. Yet most organizations stop the courtship process once somebody is hired. That's a huge mistake.

Insight of Excellence

Saying "Welcome aboard" is only the beginning.

Think about your current onboarding process for your most recent hire. Is there anything that you are expecting that employee to do at a 100% level of efficiency, right away? Usually, the answer I hear back from leaders is "yes." If that's the case, a couple of other important questions follow: Does that employee know exactly what to master in order to become great at the job? Does that employee have the ability to refer back to a playbook that contains all the relevant best practices? Does that employee know exactly when to be up-to-speed on each and every aspect of the new job? Usually, the answer I hear back from leaders on these questions is "no." That means you're in that "hire and forget" mode in which onboarding is simply not taking place—and that's a problem. Failure to onboard is a sign that your organization has not embraced and is not supporting a learning culture.

When companies don't have an onboarding process, a way to teach people what to do and what to say in order to succeed, new hires get frustrated and discouraged. They have a bad impression of the organization from the very start and lose respect for it. This has two potentially disastrous outcomes: high performers tend to leave more quickly and low performers tend to stick around longer. (All too often, low performers are "taught by the troops," a practice that may perpetuate issues you don't want to see continued.)

Recently I coached an entrepreneur who was conducting an in-depth review of different departments within his organization. His company was very successful within his industry—but it faced a challenge. There was unusually high turnover in a particular customer support function, and this high turnover rate was costing the company a lot of money. People were leaving consistently at around 12–14 months, which was a much shorter time-span than this CEO thought was acceptable. As it happened, the first major expectation set by management for this position was an assessment that tested whether the employee could meet certain performance goals. This assessment was set for right around 16 months after hiring. An unacceptably high percentage of people were bailing before they even got to that point. It occurred to me that people might just be leaving because they knew they couldn't pass the first level assessment.

We looked closely at the hiring process: It was sound, and it was being followed. So what was the issue? Was it management? Well, when we peeled back the onion, we found that this department had literally no onboarding program. Some of the people who came into the organization had relevant customer service experience; some didn't; but none of them were getting a clear sense of what they needed to do to be successful within this specific position at this organization. They didn't know the answer to the questions, "What should I learn when?" and "What do I need to do to be successful?" They had to come up with their own answers to those questions. That was a problem, because there were so many different things to learn in order to get up to speed on that particular job that most people spent the first month or two pretty confused. They didn't have a sense of the order or priority of the things that they should be learning. Because there was no onboarding process, they had to pick up whatever they could from others in the company and then follow their own intuition.

Managers would help new employees whenever they could, but they were so focused on other goals that they didn't realize there was an issue. As a result, most new employees were anxious and uncertain about where they stood and never said anything about how they felt. Who wants to say, "Hey, I have no idea what to do to be successful in your company, because I'm totally lost"? An unacceptably high number of them simply never felt comfortable within the position.

To address this problem, we identified all the areas in which new employees needed to be competent in order to succeed at their job. Once that list was created, we then put those skill areas in their order of priority. (There was no reason to learn things that you had to know in Year 2 in the first 30 days on the job.) Once we had identified the order of importance for the skill areas, we had the beginnings of our onboarding process. We gave the employees samples to replicate as they mastered those skill areas. For instance, one of the things people had to do is was place outbound "touch calls" to current customers, asking them to complete a brief survey. They had to know how to start the call, how to respond if the customer was unhappy, and so on. Without a sample to follow, everyone was doing it differently and a lot of people weren't doing it very well. This was hardly their fault since they'd simply never been trained in that skill.

As part of the onboarding process, employees now got a sample script that gave them guidance on what to say as they interacted with their customers on these calls. They also got an audio sample of a successful call that they could listen to and use as a model. Many of them listened to that recording in their car over and over until the words of the audio became their words. The new result was that the company had a much higher percentage of people answering the internal surveys and employees were more confident in their ability to perform. The company decreased turnover, saved money, and increased the ability for people to perform at a higher standard much more quickly.

Effective onboarding is essential for every new hire in every area of the organization. (Yes, this includes internal movement from one position to another.) Give people clear examples of excellence, support them, and hold them accountable for hitting measurable targets that get them closer to that standard of excellence during those first critical weeks on the job. Evaluate them along the way, and notice whenever there's a performance gap in the early days. That performance gap is a training and coaching opportunity.

Speaking of coaching, on to the next blind spot!

TAKEAWAY QUESTIONS

→ Does your organization currently have a documented onboarding process?

→ If you could implement one idea from this chapter to develop a better onboarding practice, what would it be?

→ When it comes to onboarding, in what specific, measurable area is accelerating success most important to you? Within what employee group?

9

Blind Spot: Not Knowing How to Coach

Do you know the difference between coaching and training?

Do you see steady improvement in individual and team performance?

Are you spending 35% to 40% of your time coaching?

Can your managers tell you the top two gaps that they're working on with each employee in order to help that employee improve?

Can they produce a coaching plan, based on these objectives, for the people they manage?

Do you have a coaching plan for your own direct reports?

t's easy to confuse coaching and training. Coaching is supporting employees in a one-on-one setting by asking them questions that make them aware of issues they face in implementing what they've already been trained to do. Training is imparting new skills. Notice that coaching, not training, is what enables employees to take personal responsibility for their own personal and professional development.

Coaching is both an art and a science. Ideally, managers should spend between 35% and 40% of their time coaching in support of the top ten behaviors necessary to achieve excellence within a given role, with special focus on one or two specific behaviors that represent areas for potential growth and development for a specific employee. Yet in our experience, this happens very rarely because most managers have no idea how to coach. They haven't been trained to do it, and they don't spend anywhere close to 40% of their time coaching. As a result, most people are not coached at all.

Typically, managers and leaders fall back on what they think coaching is. The manager asks a question like, "How's your week going?," and the employee responds with a story of some kind. Then the manager follows through with, "OK, got to tell you, you're off track. Here's what I would do..."

Notice that this is basically a critical parent talking to a child. No matter how comfortable you are with this kind of dialogue or how familiar it has become to you and your team, no matter what your employees may say about it, this dynamic is stressful enough for the employee to make a genuine coaching discussion impossible. There's no process guiding the discussion, no reason for the manager's initial question, and no meaningful learning experience following it.

When you're leading a real coaching session (which, by the way, always takes place in a safe, private, one-on-one setting), the objective is to empower your reports to better utilize the skills you know they have already developed, but aren't yet leveraging fully— and to support them as they identify and modify any behavior that is no longer effective. These breakthroughs must come from the ones being coached, not from you. Your job is simply to stimulate and enhance expertise in problem solving and strategic thinking. Rather than waiting to be spoon fed, your employees come to recognize their own ability to strategically tackle any challenge that comes up.

Once you understand this definition of coaching, you can see that it is a contradiction in terms to attempt to fix problems during coaching sessions. Your goal is always to encourage the other person to find the answer within. (Important note: In my own experience as a coach, I've found that my instinct to give the person the "right answer," which can be very strong, is always rooted in a desire to make myself feel important. It has nothing to do with helping the other person.)

Most so-called "coaching" meetings that leaders discuss with us are actually training sessions in disguise. They're designed to fill skill gaps. The manager does most of the talking and uses the available time to share stories and lectures on one favorite topic: "How I would deal with this." This is not coaching. Note that in a true coaching session, the coach listens at least 70% of the time and asks questions to explore potentially under-examined issues in the time that remains. The coach pursues these issues with tactful, respectful questioning until the ones being coached have a "light bulb" moment about how to implement something they already know. I'm talking about questions like, "How do you think you should respond?" And, "What are your next steps?"

Insight of Excellence

Most managers who think they're coaching someone aren't.

Recently, we were working with a senior vice president in Human Resources who shared a major challenge: Mid-level and front-line hires in her organization just didn't seem to be able to perform at a consistent level. This was true in several different departments throughout the organization. Furthermore, the largely Millennial-era workforce was leaving faster than expected, and this was having a negative financial impact on the organization. This VP had been ready to accept that Millennials could be expected leave an employer after four or five years, but the pattern that had emerged was that they were leaving her company after 12–14 months.

We did a little digging to determine what was driving these two problems. What we learned was that, although this company did a whole lot of training and teaching and sharing of information, there was literally no reinforcement and no coaching. People were being taught all kinds of good things, but they weren't sustaining any kind of meaningful learning curve that helped them lock in and utilize what they'd been taught. As a result, people were getting frustrated. They were underperforming. They were leaving early.

We set up a coaching process, one that would take employees to new levels of performance. We helped managers do a better job of helping employees move what they had learned in training into real life applications so that what they picked up in the training room could become part of what they actually did, part of their daily thought process—part of them. Over time, the managers were able to support this change and create a powerful new coaching regimen that led to improvements in morale, productivity, and retention.

You as the leader need to be coaching your individual team members often. When you do that, two important things happen: They develop and grow, and thus position themselves to make better contributions over time and, just as important, coaching becomes part of the organizational culture. Coaching is an essential management skill, and lots of leaders imagine that it's happening when it really isn't. Don't be one of them! An effective coaching process, one based on good questions, zero lecturing, and a knowledge of where the person you're coaching really wants to go in life, takes time, patience, and practice to develop. But it's worth it. (See the next blind spot.)

TAKEAWAY QUESTIONS

→ When you think of an excellent coach (using the definition of coaching shared in this chapter), who immediately comes to mind?

→ What attributes of that coach would you like to develop in yourself or in your team when it comes to coaching?

→ Do you or your organization have a fully developed coaching process and platform to develop excellence in yourself and in others? If not, what actions can you take to implement a coaching program, and when will you take these actions?

10

Blind Spot: Not Training the Management Team

What are the last three formal programs your managers attended to support their ongoing personal and professional development?

Are you sending your managers to eight days of training per year?

Do each of your managers have a personal development plan?

Do you know what the next viable career step is for each manager who reports to you?

Most of the leaders we work with wouldn't dream of hiring an accountant who had no training in accounting. They wouldn't consider for a moment hiring an engineer who had no engineering training. They'd laugh in your face if you suggested that that they receive treatment from a doctor who had no medical training. But for some reason they have no problem at all hiring or promoting someone with absolutely no management experience into a management position.

Most professionals have to go through some form of annual training to keep their skills up-to-date with the changing marketplace. Your managers should, too. So should you. Everyone should be on a constant learning journey.

When I make this point during talks and seminars, I usually see a little uncomfortable shifting around in seats from the audience. It's possible you felt a little uncomfortable just now as you read the paragraph above. If you did, that's good. Recognition is the first step toward the elimination of a blind spot. So let's continue the sometimes difficult process of recognizing blind spots whenever and wherever they arise—because this one is a big one.

Here's a gut-check question for you: How many people with zero or very little formal training in management do you currently hold responsible for managing your projects, teams, or revenue?

There's no fault in answering honestly here. Most companies have this blind spot, and if yours is a small but growing business, it's possible that any number of important people on staff (including you!) have taken on management responsibility without formal preparation or training for the job. That's what happens. The questions before you now are: What does the present look like in terms of personal and professional development for your managers? What should the future look like? To answer those questions, it helps to look closely at how this blind spot arises in the first place.

One classic example of this blind spot, and the scenario we are often called in to help company leaders remedy, is the common decision to promote a high-performing salesperson into the role of sales manager. Leaders considering such a promotion may say things to themselves like:

"How hard could the transition from salesperson to sales manager be?"

"After all, Jim is a bright guy. He already knows how to get the job done at a superior level."

"All Jim has to do is share those killer best practices of his with the rest of the team, pass along a few inspiring speeches and stories as circumstances warrant, and run a weekly pipeline meeting."

What could go wrong?

Suffice it to say a lot can, and usually does, go wrong. You do yourself, your organization, and Jim no favors when you justify this kind of decision. The two jobs are totally different.

That's just one of the most obvious examples. There are plenty of others. For instance, a fast-growing technology company we worked with had brought in, a few years back, a huge wave of hard-working managers. The problem wasn't that they weren't ready to take on the job when they were hired. The problem was that, over time, they needed more support from the organization than they were getting.

As we looked at what was going on in their organization, we saw that all the different parts of the organization were growing dramatically—but not the skill level of the front-line managers, nor the support to get the right training and tools. The regulatory environment was changing, the marketplace was changing, and there was heavy global competition. In response to these challenges, senior management was doing tons of research and development, investing in lots of product training, and focusing heavily on the development of front-line employees—but there was no ongoing management training.

Insight of Excellence

Managers—your company's future senior leaders—must be personally invested in their own learning and development.

I made the case that the managers, the company's future senior leaders, needed to be invested in their own learning and development. They needed to spend eight to ten days per year on their own personal development, on finding ways to improve their work life, to increase their own personal effectiveness on the job and to keep up with the changes in the industry. Senior management agreed with me that this was an investment worth making, and over time we saw some dramatic positive results in a number of different areas.

First and foremost, the managers felt better about their ability to do their job and about their relationship with the company. That meant they were more likely to stick around, and less likely to be poached by the competition. Second, they were leading their teams with greater confidence and conviction, which made a huge difference in both morale and productivity. Last but certainly not least, they upped their game. They started regular one-on-one coaching sessions with each of their people, which was a huge step forward, and they also got better at setting expectations and having difficult conversations with underperforming team members who needed to change their approach to their job or move on. The change was rapid, and it reverberated at all levels of the organization. Once the managers had upgraded their skills, life at that organization got substantially better for both the frontline employee and the manager.

That's what can happen—but it usually doesn't. Most managers, in our experience, do not receive basic management training or reinforcement. They often go into the job without any kind of training program that teaches them how to excel in every aspect of their job. They never get a playbook. They're in "sink or swim" mode. They themselves were not coached and developed properly so even though there are plenty of people they can emulate, they don't have a framework for coaching and developing the people who report to them.

That's a shame, because management is the most difficult job on the chart in most organizations. If you're a manager, you have customer issues, employee issues, and senior management issues that you're juggling at all times. In fact, every manager really has four different jobs, four different hats to wear: coach, trainer, supervisor, and mentor. The reality is that most managers come into a management job without a lot of training ahead of time in any of these areas. They have learned to figure out some things as they go along, but inevitably there are gaps. Senior management needs to step up and take its share of responsibility for identifying these gaps and, if possible, filling them.

As a leader, your ultimate goal has to be to make sure that you support your team, that you give your team the things necessary for them to succeed. That means you need to look closely at your own management team—including, but not limited to, sales managers—and to ask yourself some tough questions. Specifically:

→ What kind of training do your managers need to do their job at a level of excellence?
→ What kind of coaching do they need going forward?
→ Who should be doing that coaching?

If there is no formal coaching process in place in your organization and no personal development plan in place for each manager (and indeed for each employee!), then that's a major blind spot.

Most organizations don't address this blind spot. Somehow they have let their managers move away from people management and into paper management. Many have been allowed to believe they are responsible, first and foremost, for spreadsheets and printouts and the numbers that show up on them. That's not true. They are responsible for managing and growing people. Managers have to take full responsibility for helping their people grow. That starts with the managers themselves.

The positive results will show up more quickly than you may expect. I was working recently with an organization whose senior leadership could not understand why its managers were not doing what they were expected to do—why they were performing poorly. We did an analysis. Surprise, surprise: Senior management had unrealistic expectations because the managers had literally never been trained to do the jobs they were expected to do. That's quite common, as I've suggested. There's this unhealthy assumption in many organizations that, just because people have the word "manager" in their job title, they either know everything or can know everything in a matter of minutes. It's just not true.

Once we trained the managers and set up a realistic reinforcement and coaching plan, the picture got a lot brighter. A few months later, the managers were doing a fantastic job—and the company was back on track.

TAKEAWAY QUESTIONS

→ What kind of training and reinforcement do your managers need to perform their jobs at a level of excellence? How will they get that training and reinforcement?

→ Are managers currently required to attend trainings that their teams attend, or is that attendance optional?

→ Why is it important for managers to attend and fully participate in the training programs in which their teams participate?

11

Blind Spot: Not Focusing on Lead Generation

How many total new conversations does your sales team need in a given week in order for them to hit your quota this quarter?

Does your compensation plan reward the right behaviors?

Are your experienced people selling net new business?

Are you getting the right types of leads from your marketing team?

L ead generation is the lifeblood of any business. It's one of those things people tend to think happens miraculously, thanks to elves who come into the office at night, leave before people show up the next morning, and set all the appointments. Unfortunately, lead generation does not take care of itself. If lead generation is not an organizational priority, there is always crisis on the horizon.

As the individual producers in your company grow from new hires to seasoned veterans, one of the first things that a lot of them will drop from their routine is prospecting. Yet if you talk to the most successful people in the sales world, they'll tell you that even at the peak of their careers, when they are making millions of dollars, they still spend a portion of their time prospecting for new business. This is the way it should be. This is how salespeople should prioritize their time. But it's not the way most salespeople operate.

The blind spot that most leaders have is that they tend to focus on the wrong end of the funnel. They focus on the lagging indicators, like closed sales, and ignore the leading indicators, the behaviors that make those sales possible. They fixate on questions like: "What's closing in the next 30 days?" When they ask a question like that, they're only paying attention to things that are in the middle and at the end of the sales funnel. They're not looking where they really need to look.

Leaders need to look at what's going into the funnel to find out whether what's happening there is healthy enough to sustain their business. If the people on your sales team have a healthy amount of qualified opportunities going into the funnel, a lot of good things happen. You have less stress, you don't have to negotiate away your margins, and you are less vulnerable to the problem of having to worry about whether one or two things in the funnel are going to close.

Most organizations are focused on quotas that are based on what's happening in the middle or at the end of the sales funnel, and they're not looking upstream. That's a mistake. Knowing what's just about to close is important, of course, but it doesn't tell you what is next. The sales funnel is always hungry, and it must be fed. The most successful salespeople spend a large portion of their time generating new opportunities; they are laser-focused on their ratios. They know that when their ratios go down, the organization suffers and they suffer.

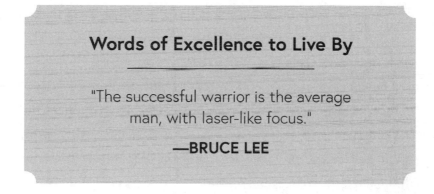

Words of Excellence to Live By

"The successful warrior is the average man, with laser-like focus."

—BRUCE LEE

So you need to start a different conversation. You need to ask your team, "How many net new conversations do we need every single week in order to hit our numbers?"

There will be a blank stare at first, and that's OK. At least you've begun the conversation. Now you can spend the time identifying the top ten ways you can drive net new leads into your organization. Once you know what those behaviors are, you can start looking at a whole different set of questions. For instance, you can ask whether you have invested enough time in a given prospecting activity. Is the frequency of that activity high enough? Can you get better at executing it? You should also ask: Does your compensation program match the outcome you want your team to deliver?

Does your compensation program pay based on revenue, or does it pay based on how you got the revenue? For instance, should net new business be paid at a higher commission rate than revenue from existing business? Should the behaviors that lead to revenue generate some kind of a commission, not just the deal crossing the finish line?

When the funnel is light, people tend to make bad decisions. They tend to keep throwing resources at a deal that was never going to be closed—or they discount heavily in order to get the deal. That's not where you want to be!

One company we worked with on this lead generation issue was in the chemical additive business. The sales team was dealing with huge, destabilizing swings in its sales performance—the classic "peaks and valleys" problem. This company did business primarily through referral sources and second-tier sales; its salespeople went on a lot of joint calls, although they also made many calls on their own. The members of the team were successful, but not as successful as they could be. That's because they were basically reactive, and as a result they had to deal with huge income swings.

Both the salespeople and the team leaders were focusing on the accounts that were in the funnel. They all wanted to know: What would it take to go from Step 1 to Step 2 with such-and-such an account? When would this happen? How much should be forecasted? How could they get that prospect to drop out the other end of the funnel as a sale?

All the discussion, all the focus, was on those accounts that were already in the individual's sales funnel. That kind of discussion is necessary, of course, but it shouldn't get all the attention.

What we were able to do was help them put more of the focus on the front of the funnel, on the pre-sale activity. After working with us, the members of the sales team instituted a process that would help them make sure that they were always filling up their funnel, always proactively looking to make sure that the behaviors and activities constantly fed the front end of the prospecting funnel.

Yes, there was always a certain amount of pressure on the funnel to close deals. That's understandable. But the point is, we were also able to focus their time, energy, and metrics on the number of net new prospects coming into the funnel. As they did that, they found they had fewer ups and downs. Their inventory management was also much better because they could plan based on a steady, predictable flow of new business. By creating an effective up-front prospecting process, both of those issues were solved.

That's the kind of approach you need to take. At the very least, all members of your sales team need to be able to tell you how many net new conversations they need this month in order to hit their quarterly or annual quota. At the very least, you need to create a prospecting plan for each employee who generates revenue through getting new customers. In setting up this plan, you need to bear in mind that prospecting doesn't just mean net new customers you haven't done business with before; it also could be net new business within your existing customer base.

Remember: You have a constant need for new business in the funnel. A salesperson who simply stops prospecting usually won't even notice the shortfall for six to eight weeks. Think about that! That's a long time to imagine you're on the right track when you're not. Typically, we find that salespeople need a minimum of two net new conversations per day, each concluding in a scheduled next step, to be successful. If you're looking for a universal standard that will be relevant to each member of your team responsible for generating new business, you could do a lot worse than to start there.

Focus your team on generating net new opportunities. Focus on the front of the funnel, and the middle and end of the funnel will take care of themselves.

(For more on this important topic, check out my podcast at www.sandler.com/sandler.com/resources/webinars/stressless-prospecting-the-sandler-way.)

TAKEAWAY QUESTIONS

→ Which lead-generation behaviors (leading indicators) do you monitor in assessing the daily performance of your sales team?

→ On a scale of 1 to 10, with 10 being best, how effective is your team today at filling the funnel?

→ What messaging needs to be delivered within your organization when it comes to lead generation?

12

Blind Spot: No Methodologies and Systems

Do you have systems and processes for the important things that happen in your business (for instance, acquiring a customer and managing that customer's experience)?

Do you hold people accountable for following these systems?

Many leaders I talk to tell me that they're tired of worrying about how things are getting done or being told they're micromanaging their people when all they're really doing is sharing the right way to do something. Others tell me they're tired of asking people to start thinking for themselves and taking the initiative—and not seeing any change in behavior. All three groups of leaders are complaining about the same thing, though they may not realize it: a lack of effective methodologies and systems.

People need to know where they can drive. They need to know

where the authority "guardrails" on the road are. They want to know where they have the freedom to operate using their own best judgment and where they don't. Here's the key point: Either the process shows people where the guardrails are, or you do. It shouldn't be you!

Your people should be crystal clear about the process they're supposed to follow. Their individual creativity and excellence will come through best when they know how to do a good job by following a well-designed process, not when they're depending on you for a decision. If they're always looking to you for a decision and they come to depend on that, then it doesn't matter how often you tell them to think for themselves and take action. They will always come back to you. Whether they realize what they're doing or not, they will try to make their success your responsibility. If you've ever had direct reports ask for your "feedback" on something they are uncertain about how to finish—an employee evaluation, say—you know what I'm talking about. This is a symptom of a lack of process. If you end up writing the evaluation or contributing to it substantially, you're making the problem worse.

The good news is, you've probably already got some parts of your business that have clear processes in place. Some corners of the organization (such as shipping) have probably evolved good processes by default; other departments will need more conscious effort to identify a process that people can follow. Some departments in your organization will have big-picture processes and methodologies in place, but for the day-to-day operations they won't have much of anything. Most organizations we work with find that the ability to create clear, workable processes throughout the organization—from the leader's office on down—is an important leadership priority and a marker of organizational growth. Note how different this is from the common pattern where leaders follow a "process" that exists only in their head. (By the way, in case you were wondering, there is an ideal excellence process for leaders; it has six clear steps, which we call the Six P's, and it repeats in a cycle that never ends. It is laid out in Part Two of this book.)

The big challenge leaders face here is that they usually don't know what other people don't know. They may assume, because of their own level of competency, that everybody has all the information needed to do the job well, and that's a mistake. Leaders need to be sure there's a process in place for everyone, and they need to find a way to confirm that their processes are up-to-date.

One great place to start when you're creating or improving a process is to ask new employees—people who have been with you for 90 days or less—what information and guidance they wish they'd had during those first months. Was there anything they had to learn on their own that they wished they hadn't? What didn't they have that they wished they'd had, as far as directions and processes were concerned? What could you have done that would have made it easier for them? The answers you get can tell you a lot about the processes you need to implement or revise. There's always something you as an organization can do better, some area that has been forgotten. I make a point of taking new employees out for lunch at or around their 60-day mark, and I can tell you I always learn a great deal about how we can improve our processes.

It may be tempting to respond to this blind spot by saying something like, "Hang on. This sounds like a lot of trouble. Nobody was there to hold my hand or write out a process for me when I was doing that job, and I did all right. Why can't my people just collaborate, think for themselves, and find the best way forward on their own, like I did?" Saying this, or even thinking it, may feel good, but it leaves out an important part of the leadership equation. Leaders are extremely passionate about what they do. What they're really saying here is, "Why aren't people as passionate about this business as I am?" The best answer to that question is: It's not their business. It's your business. The culture you instill and support in the organization can certainly help you and your team address this issue in the longer term—but before you even get there, you need to come to terms with the reality that it's your responsibility to meet people where they are and to support them by giving them the information and guidance they need to deliver a consistent result for you.

The response that says, "They're smart; they can figure it out," is counterproductive. You need to accept that it's your job to think closely about the different segments of your business—sales, customer service, manufacturing, accounting, engineering, whatever— and identify all the important processes within that. So, for instance, in the sales function, you have processes like, "How do we find new prospects to talk to?" and "How do we turn those prospects into customers?" You need to build up the lists in all of the critical areas. Then, after you have identified all the elements, you need to ask yourself if you have written processes and systems in place that support your people so they can execute at the level of excellence.

In addition to meeting with new employees and getting their feedback, sit down with your team at least once a quarter to come up with areas where you could do a better job creating or upgrading methodologies and processes. Ask them: "What are the most important functions that we carry out?" "How do we do that?" "Is there a written process for doing that?" "If so, how up-to-date is it, and how useful is it?" "If not, what's the best way for us to create a written process?" I also like to ask new (and veteran) employees what I call the "well, better, different" questions: "What do you think we do well?" "What could we do better?" "What do we need to do differently?" There should be processes for acting on and implementing the best answers to each of these questions.

Insight of Excellence

Ask these questions constantly: "What do we do well? What could we do better? What do we need to do differently?"

Of course, many people will resist process, and because of that, you may be tempted to give up. Don't. Overcoming this blind spot means accepting that process is what allows you to be successful regardless of who's doing what job. Process is what allows you to find out exactly where you're dropping the ball and what to do about it. Process is really the equivalent of an MRI in the medical world. It replaces exploratory surgery. The surgeons could open you up on the operating table and hope they find the problem, which is what most businesses do, or they could put you through an MRI and identify exactly where the issue is before they take action. Which would you prefer? You can do the same thing with systems and processes because, if you do it right, you'll know exactly where the cause-and-effect relationships are. If the effect is not what you want in a specific area, you have the chance to look objectively at what caused that outcome.

Let me give you a personal example of implementing process. My family has a vacation home that all the kids can go to on their own. I have a mental checklist of items I have to do to open and close the house. In the beginning, when people first started using the vacation home, the kids either didn't know or forgot all the things that had to be done to open up and close. They did the best they could, but there was always something they forgot to do. I created a process—a written checklist—for opening and closing the house, based on what I had done and improved upon over the years. Thanks to that checklist, the opening and closing of the vacation house is now a no-brainer. We update the checklist as needed. It's easy to understand, everybody follows it, and all the stress of opening and closing the house (not to mention the stress of worrying about whether something important has been forgotten) is gone for good.

Documenting systems and methodologies and keeping them up-to-date may seem like extra work. It's not. It's saving everyone extra work. When systems and methodologies are established and pursued properly—not as a weapon, but as an enhancement—you'll always see the dividends along the way.

TAKEAWAY QUESTIONS

→ What is a methodology or system in your organization that is currently being followed and is proving highly effective? Why is that particular methodology or system effective?

→ When was the last time your team evaluated existing methodologies and systems?

→ If you could isolate one methodology or system that you believe needs updating to drive excellence in your organization, which one would it be? Why?

13

Blind Spot: Not Implementing Organizational Change Initiatives Effectively

Have you addressed the concerns of key stakeholders and incorporated their feedback before launching your plan?

Have you identified internal allies who will help you make the change you want a reality?

Have you developed an effective reinforcement strategy?

Changes in your market. Changes in technology. Changes in the economy. Changes in the regulatory landscape. Changes in your team's composition or structure that affect people's ability to do their jobs. As a leader, you may not see these big things coming, but you have to prepare for them as best you can and help your team prepare. That's a huge and important part of your job.

Words of Excellence to Live By

"Change, before you have to."

—JACK WELCH

Here's the challenge, though. When you do come up with a plan for dealing with the change on the horizon by creating a change initiative of your own, what usually happens? You get pushback.

Organizational change, whether it takes the form of a change in the bonus plan, a change in the management team, or anything in between, is one of those things that you may spend a lot of time preparing for and then not like the results you get once you share your decision with the rest of the team.

Here's what this blind spot looks like. You've spent an incredible amount of time thinking about a certain issue, you've committed yourself to thinking about all the possible responses to that problem, and then you simply dictate the solution to the rest of the organization. Typically, you might do this by sending out a memo that says, "This is the change that we're about to implement in so-and-so area. Effective such-and-such a date, the new policy is X, Y, and Z. Thank you for your cooperation." You then mark the item off your to-do list, thinking that the hard work is now done, that your marching orders have been made clear, and that the memo will do the rest of the diplomatic work for you. But it doesn't. What you think of as the end of the discussion is only the beginning for someone who hasn't been involved.

The unfortunate reality may be that no one even understands why the change was necessary in the first place. People may not yet have a clear sense of the effect the change will have on them personally. They are likely to assume the worst. When that happens, people and teams seize up. The disconnects between what you wanted to happen in the organization and what actually happens get wider and wider. Suddenly you're not dealing with the change initiative, but with a whole host of new miscommunication issues related to it. This happens because you haven't done a good job educating people about what you're doing and why you're doing it. You didn't design the roll-out well.

Here are the three areas to focus in on when it comes to designing and implementing change initiatives.

1. All the necessary pre-activity before the change must be identified and communicated. This includes talking to user groups ahead of time about what kind of change is being contemplated, why it is being contemplated, and what the impact on people is likely to be. What you hear from these stakeholders should affect the design of the implementation plan. To the degree that it's possible, let them shape the approach to the change.

2. The implementation of the change initiative itself must be carefully designed and managed. As a practical matter, this means multiple communication formats, including face-to-face meetings (as opposed to firing off a single email to the

entire company at eleven o'clock at night and thinking, "My work here is done"). People should get video explaining what's happening, audio explaining what's happening, and in-person discussions that explain what's happening. During implementation, you will certainly want to explain to the group exactly what the change is, what the driving reasons behind the change are, and how your response to the change has taken into consideration the views of all of those who are affected or will be affected by the change. Make absolutely sure that you've communicated very clearly, in multiple formats, all the key issues that arose when you talked to your user groups. In addition, identify specific people on your team who can speak to suggestions about how best to relate to the change, people who can share their excitement about what the future looks like with the proposed response to change that you're rolling out. I like to think of these people as managers of change, or MOCs. They're the ones who will be leading by example, the early adopters who have already embraced the fact that the change will be a better thing. They need to be part of your initial messaging about the change. Don't just announce what's happening on your own. Understand that you're at about the 70-yard line on this initiative, while everyone else in the organization is back at about the two-yard line. They need information and help. They need people who can get them up to speed and serve as role models.

3. The reinforcement of the message has to be effective. After you launch the initiative, you have to do reality checks.

Create meetings where small groups get to talk about how the change initiative has made things better, based on the initial problem. During those meetings, ask about things that could be adjusted to make the change initiative even better. Continue to celebrate people who have gotten out front and who are leading by example; share as many of their success stories as you can, again through multiple communication channels. In short, find ways to constantly reinforce the message. You can't just check this off the to-do list. People need to experience a message four or five times in order for it to become reality in their daily lives; they usually won't change their behavior based on a single message. Usually, they'll take a "wait and see" approach. Maybe the change you're talking about implementing will fall into the "this too shall pass" category. They'll look for evidence that you're really serious. By setting up an effective reinforcement plan and making sure that the change is continually talked about, you send a message to the organization that this is not going to go away and that people should participate in the change. Expect to spend some time on this.

We recently had a major change at our organization concerning the launch of a new online training platform. Getting the word out about it and answering people's questions took two separate videos, a series of weekly webinars, any number of informal person-to-person Q&A sessions, and a special podcast. All in all, we spent five months following up on this change initiative. But it was time well spent because the change was successful.

TAKEAWAY QUESTIONS

→ Think of a recent major change that took place within your organization. What activities or messaging took place prior to that change?

→ Before the change was implemented, was change readiness taken into consideration?

→ Can you think of any ways the change management process could have been handled more effectively?

14

Blind Spot: Not Sharing the Vision with Those Tasked with Implementing It

Do you have a vision for your company's future?

If you asked five employees, at random, to write down the vision of your company, would their answers cohere, or would they present radically different versions of your company's vision?

Can your people accurately describe the value of the project they are working on and how it fits into the mission?

U nderstanding and helping to implement the corporate vision, whether it's the owner's vision or the executive vision, is inspiring to everyone. As a leader, it's your job to make sure those who are supposed to carry out your vision understand what it is.

Most employees really do want to know the answer to the

question "Where are we headed over the next X years?" if only from a point of self-interest. They want to know what their own career possibilities are going to look like. So paint a picture for them. Set a target. Let people know where you want to go. Share a dream that captures the imagination, like Dr. Martin Luther King, Jr.'s dream of a future where people were judged by the content of their character or John F. Kennedy's dream to send a man to the moon before the decade of the 1960s was out.

It's worth noting that when Kennedy made that challenge, the United States' record in space was distinctly lackluster. The country had only the Alan Shepard Freedom 7 flight to point to as a success. That mission, the first manned American flight into space, did not complete a single orbit of the Earth; it had been preceded by the Russian Yuri Gagarin's historic mission, which was the first to send a human being into space. Yet, even though there was no great record to point to yet, there was something about the scale and emotion of Kennedy's challenge that captivated the country, challenged its imagination and its people, and inspired it to achieve much greater things—as indeed it did. Corporate challenges to the imagination, and to people, can work in much the same way.

When you publicly dream as Kennedy and King dreamed, you allow people to get creative and enroll themselves as collaborators in your vision. So talk about your vision often. Create and share a compelling vision of where your company is going. Once you've done that, you can start to paint the picture of what you and your people are going to need to do to get from where you are today to the place where that vision will eventually bring you.

Words of Excellence to Live By

"The more boundless your vision,
the more real you are."

—DEEPAK CHOPRA

The blind spot in this area is pretty basic: Leaders tend not to have a complete vision—or, if they do, they tend to keep it to themselves or share it only within the ranks of management. These are big mistakes. When people don't know what your vision is, it's hard for them to find a way make it their own.

The leader's goal should always be to make the vision "ours" as opposed to "mine." Make sure yours is easy for everyone to embrace. Make it easy for people to discuss the vision, get excited about it, and share their own suggestions about it. If there are areas where people want to propose additions and upgrades, don't let your ego get in the way. Listen to what people have to say, and be ready to upgrade the vision as circumstances require. Talk about the plans people suggest, identify the very best ones, and identify the specific goals and the metrics that support those plans. Get people working on projects to help you all get to where you're all going, and keep on sharing the vision. Keep everybody updated in every meeting about the progress you're making. Say things like, "Here are the three projects that we're working on in order for us to hit our vision."

When you make a habit of this, you'll find that the "we" voice starts to take precedence over the "me" voice in your company's discussions. You'll find that when you share the plans, people will become accountable for turning them into reality. You'll find that people who share and are aligned with your vision for the company are helping you evangelize on behalf of it.

Recently, I was coaching a very successful entrepreneur; she truly cared about the future of her organization and it showed. The business was doing very well. But, she was trying to pivot the firm into additional areas of expertise that would, within three years, transform her organization from a regional success into a national success. That was her vision. The challenge was, this transition wasn't happening fast enough. Her people were resisting. They didn't understand what the next phase of the company's development looked like, and as a result they didn't follow through on key initiatives.

To put it bluntly, some of the entrepreneur's people didn't see the importance of moving the company to the next level. They didn't understand or buy into the decision she had made for the business. Why not? Simple answer: She hadn't started that conversation. She hadn't allowed her own people to contribute to the discussion. She hadn't listened to them.

Through coaching discussions, the entrepreneur came to her own conclusions about the best ways to close that gap. She realized that her owning the vision was not enough. Once she started communicating more effectively about the vision she was already living, day in and day out, and once she started enrolling people, telling them where they fit and listening to their questions about that vision, her team started to understand what the end game looked like and how they would benefit from it. It was at that point that they started participating with full engagement in the "How do we get there?" discussion.

Suddenly it wasn't just the entrepreneur's goals that were on the table—it was "our implementation plan." Because the entrepreneur had improved her communication, because she did a better job of setting and reinforcing the vision, her team was able to make the transition from "what you want" to "what we want." People understood their own role in the huge change that was about to take place, and they began to make proactive suggestions that the founder of the business could never have come up with on her own. They ended up completing the pivot she envisioned in just 14 months. That would never have been possible if she hadn't effectively shared, communicated, and reinforced the vision she had for her company.

A company without a constantly reinforced corporate vision is an organization without a GPS. Without that vision, you're going to go in circles—and ultimately, you're going to run out of gas.

TAKEAWAY QUESTIONS

→ Does everyone in the organization know the company's mission, values, and goals?

→ How is the vision currently shared?

→ What specific actions can you take today to make sure that the vision is communicated in such a way that everyone in the company can understand and support it?

15

The Blind Spots and the Four Kinds of Businesses, Revisited

As seen in the prior chapters, those, then, are the blind spots. They are the symptoms of an impending or current downward spiral for your business. You'll recall that, a little earlier in the book, we divided businesses into four categories: at-risk, average, well-managed, and excellent.

→ **At-risk** businesses display every single one of the blind spots I just shared with you. They fall prey to the downward slide I call the blind-spots syndrome, and as a result, their long-term survival is an open question.

→ **Average** businesses are likely to suffer from five to eight of the blind spots you've just read about. The thing to understand about average businesses is that they are always on the brink of slipping into the at-risk zone. Complacent leadership is typically the culprit here. If these businesses don't adapt and find a way to move out of their comfort zones, their growth potential is limited.

→ **Well-managed** businesses suffer from between one and four of the blind spots you've just read about. Perhaps 20–30% of the companies we've worked with could be classified as well-managed organizations. Well-managed companies are doing a lot of things right, and they may even be market leaders. But they, too, may be stuck in one or more comfort zones—familiar ways of running the business that have worked in the past.

→ **Excellent** businesses do not suffer from any of the blind spots for long periods of time. They follow a process that allows them to constantly review each of the blind spot areas to make sure they don't appear. If they do appear, leadership takes quick action. They've familiarized themselves with these issues ahead of time and built the best responses into a sound management system. As a result, they don't get blindsided in any of these classic trouble areas.

Maybe you're wondering: How, exactly, do these leaders manage to avoid, overcome, and prevent these blind spots? The answer lies in six powerful, sequential leadership strategy focus points that leaders at these companies have used to build a truly bulletproof business.

PART TWO

The Excellence Process

The Six P's

I n examining what else organizations of excellence have in common, we've found that, overall, there are six big-picture strategic factors they all manage to turn into action steps. Implementing all six of these steps in order and making them part of your culture turns excellence into a process—and gets rid of the blind spots.

Words of Excellence to Live By

"We are what we repeatedly do. Excellence, then, is not an act, but a habit."

—WILL DURANT

We call these six steps the "Excellence Process" or the "Six P's." Take a look.

1. **Planning.** Excellence starts with planning. Organizations do not to rise to the top by accident. Great leaders have a vision for themselves and their organizations. They define the mission and values necessary to take the organization to their vision. They assess the environment and what it takes to grow, then create the plans to get there, knowing all along that they will constantly reassess their position.

2. **Positions.** Leaders at companies of excellence have created the proper organizational structure and determined the skills required for each of the positions within that

structure. If those positions don't exist, they create them. Leaders of these companies have identified a company structure capable of leading the organization to fulfillment of their vision.

3. **People.** Leaders of companies of excellence know how to determine who, of the current employees, fits into the vision-driven company structure—and who doesn't. They recruit and hire new employees with the skills needed to contribute quickly to success.

4. **Processes.** Excellence leaders have created processes for nearly everything that occurs on an ongoing basis. Great leaders follow clearly documented, step-by-step processes for more consistent outcomes and expect and demand that their employees do the same.

5. **Performetrics.** Great leaders excel at holding themselves and their employees accountable to do the specific activities that lead to successful performance within a given function. When these activities are agreed upon, tracked, monitored, and discussed, people stay focused on the right things. This is what keeps organizations in the excellent category.

6. **Passion.** Great leaders have a passion to take their organization to the excellent category—and keep it there. They have figured out how to make sure the whole team has the passion they have. They have found ways to share that passion throughout the organization—particularly with future leaders as they emerge.

16

Beyond Treating the Symptoms

The blind spots you've read about are all symptoms of problems within a business. The biggest reason business leaders advance to the excellent category is their willingness to move beyond treating only symptoms by constantly attacking the underlying causes.

Words of Excellence to Live By

"We often preoccupy ourselves with the symptoms, whereas if we went to the root cause of the problems, we would be able to overcome the problems once and for all."

—WANGARA MAATHAI

The best way to do this is to follow all six of the steps laid out in Chapters 16–22, over and over and over again, as a way of business and a way of living. This is the Excellence Process. As I've mentioned, the Excellence Process has six clear steps, and it repeats in a cycle that literally never ends.

Specifically, leaders of organizations of excellence are willing to:

→ Make planning a constant feature of their personal routine and their organization's daily operational culture. They understand that planning prevents poor performance, and they build the planning step into everything they do. They plan the quarter, the week, the day, the meeting—everything. They truly believe that preparation increases the odds of success, and they act accordingly.

→ Take the time to create the proper organizational structure. This means matching the organizational chart to the mission.

→ Invest in employees who have the skills required to go to the next level. Leaders know that people are the ultimate resource.

→ Create clear, documented processes for just about everything that happens in the business. Leaders know that people can't be expected to do their jobs unless they have a process to follow.

→ Hold the leaders themselves and others in the organization accountable by means of customized, quantifiable metrics. These numbers track behaviors and outcomes that are completely under the control of the individual whose metrics are being followed.

→ Make the leaders' own passion for growing the business

contagious. They make excellence a never-ending journey and enroll others in the possibility of taking that journey with them.

In pursuing these six essential steps, leaders of organizations of excellence spend far more time working on the business than they do solving narrow operational problems in the business. They adopt a truly strategic focus.

Most leaders, however, don't adopt such a focus. As a result, their teams struggle and they themselves experience far more stress than they should. Their businesses bounce back and forth between the average and at-risk categories. This second half of the book is your opportunity to choose which group of leaders you want to belong to: those who choose excellence or those who choose to follow the path of least resistance. The hard but important truth I have to share with you now is that you can't belong to both groups. You have to pick one or the other.

Here are some typical comments we hear from business leaders who have not yet chosen excellence and whose business model, whether they realize it or not, is the path of least resistance:

→ "I'm so burdened by my job that I haven't seen any of my children's ball games."
→ "I keep having to correct errors that my employees are making."
→ "Why am I the only one still at my desk after 5:00?"
→ "My business partner doesn't work as hard as I do."
→ "It seems like all I do is put out fires every day."
→ "Planning just isn't a priority in our organization."

→ "We have employees who just don't fit into our culture."

→ "My spouse is tired of hearing me complain about work."

→ "The business isn't doing well financially, and I'm not really sure why."

→ "I'm supposed to be a leader, but it doesn't seem like anyone is following me!"

Like the blind spots I shared with you in Part One, the statements you just read are not the real issues these business owners face. They are symptoms of problems that can only be corrected through an effective, ongoing system of professional management.

You need to address the root cause if you want a permanent solution. For example, consider those who are significantly overweight and have elected to undergo gastric bypass surgery. After the procedure, some patients choose not to alter their lifestyles and eating habits. As a result, they regain the weight, once again endangering their health. The surgery was a temporary solution, but did not address the root cause, which may have been an eating disorder that should have been treated by a medical professional who specializes in that field.

In much the same way, business leaders often engage consultants to help them overcome problems in a specific area. For example, if they are not happy with their recruiting efforts, they might bring in a specialist to help them recruit, hire, and train the right people. All too often, though, after the consultant leaves, things gradually revert back to the way they were. The business leaders move out of recruiting mode. Why? Because leadership in the organization is not strong enough to sustain the discipline and accountability that had been established in that area with the consultant's help—or perhaps because the consultant didn't give the company the tools necessary to be self-sufficient in that area.

Whatever the reason, company leaders slip back into old habits simply because they treated the change as a "check the box" activity. They think, "OK, we dealt with it, we paid the consultant, so now let's move on to the next project." But they don't make a systematic change in the way they approach running the business.

That's the problem. All they did was treat the symptoms—for a while. They never actually removed the cause of the blind spots that threatened their business.

Simply treating the symptoms isn't the best answer. The better approach is to adopt a comprehensive professional management system you can use to run your organization effectively, day after day, week after week, month after month, quarter after quarter. An organization that is truly professionally managed has built-in checks and balances that enable it to identify and eradicate its blind spots and remain stable, even in the most unstable business environments.

Of course, there have been many books and articles written about professional management systems, some more academic than others. The common thread that unites all of them is that there must be systems in place if your goal is to maintain control and balance and make success sustainable.

Unfortunately, most businesses are not led by people who choose excellence as a way of life. Most business leaders opt for quick fix after quick fix in order to survive, much like the temporary relief of a cortisone injection. At first it might be hard to understand why any organization would not want to choose excellence, but the reason is more obvious than you might think. It takes a lot of work and change for an organization to become truly professionally managed. In fact, few leaders have the desire or courage to make a personal commitment to ensuring that the right changes happen.

If you want to become one of those leaders; if you want to move beyond treating the symptoms; if you want to make the blind-spots syndrome a thing of the past; if you want to commit to building an organization of excellence—keep reading. You're about to get a closer look at the Six P's, the signposts on the road to excellence.

17

Planning

Planning is a perpetual process for leaders of organizations of excellence.

Planning is not a one-time or periodic event for effective leaders. It's not something to be checked off the to-do list, but rather a continuous and constantly renewed process. It's a way of doing business.

Leaders at excellent companies run their business using planning as an integral part of what they do, every single day, without exception. For them, planning is not a project. It's part of their DNA.

While these leaders might go off-site annually to encourage others on the team to take a fresh look at the plan as part of a scheduled deep review, they don't really have to re-familiarize themselves with the core elements of the current plan for the simple reason that they've adopted perpetual planning as a way of life. Not only that: They already have the necessary business controls (budgets, forecasts, dashboards, and so on) in place to monitor performance against the plan on a daily basis. As a result, they don't fall into the common pattern of at-risk and average organizations: spending loads of time on account plans, strategic plans, and implementation plans—often with cool code names such as "Operation Streamline" or "Best-in-the-Industry Battle Plan"—only to file them all in a binder on the shelf and leave them totally unexamined until the same time next year. That's when the so-called "annual planning" process begins again. That's not planning. That's pretending to plan. If planning is something you only do once a year or once a quarter, you have not yet taken the first step on the road to excellence.

Insight of Excellence

The right plan is never written in stone for the simple reason that even the best assumptions can turn out to be dead wrong or significantly off course.

The reason for the necessity of perpetual planning is simple. New circumstances constantly arise. These invariably require the plan to be modified and, in some cases, re-written entirely. Since change is a constant in business (and in life), planning is best understood as an ongoing process that is vital to both personal and organizational success. Even superior plans are off course roughly 90% of the time. You can know with certainty where you are now and you can know exactly where you're going—but you can also be sure that your plan is slightly off and is going to need adjusting along the way.

How far ahead should your strategic plan look? For the majority of privately held businesses, a plan that looks three years forward is sufficient, if it truly becomes a perpetual planning process that continuously looks out over the next 36 months. Notice how different this is from the common approach of *only* taking a fresh look at the plan every 36 months!

There are plenty of exceptions to the 36-month standard, though, and you must plan according to the realities of your own business environment. In industries like pharmaceuticals, the time horizon is likely to be significantly further out. In a more rapidly shifting field, such as software development, the planning window might actually be a little shorter, due to the brief product life cycle, which reflects the time before the next version of the technology must be released. Regardless of how many years the plan looks forward, it should be reviewed and revised at least annually.

The Six P's: Your Action Sequence Matters

When it comes to planning (as in so much else in business, and in life) the order in which you decide to take action is extremely important. Within each of the Six P's, I'll be sharing specific best practices that outline not just what the most effective leaders do to take their organizations into the excellent category and keep them there, but the sequence in which they do those things.

Notice that planning itself precedes everything else in this management system. It's the first P for a reason. If the best practices I'm sharing with you in this chapter aren't implemented in the order described, then there's no use moving on to the second P (Positions) or indeed any of the other leadership initiatives we'll be looking at together in this book.

Here are the planning best practices we'll examine in this chapter.

→ Developing a personal vision.

→ Creating the organizational vision, mission, values, and beliefs.

→ Analyzing the external environment.

→ Conducting a SWOT analysis.

→ Revisiting the organizational vision.

→ Identifying key priorities.

→ Establishing clear expectations for each key priority.

→ Setting action items, due dates, and assignment of responsibilities.

→ Allocating resources to accomplish action plans.

→ Conducting regular planning reviews.

Excellence Best Practice: Developing a Personal Vision

Leaders develop a compelling personal vision of where they want to go in life.

If you own the company, your personal vision must serve as the foundation of the later organizational plan you create for the company. If you don't own the company, your personal vision should be in harmony with both the corporate mission you inherit and the organizational plan you set up for your team.

Michael owns ABC Engineering Company. He and his wife Joan have spent a lot of time discussing Michael's personal vision for ABC, and have also had discussions with their two children, Natalie and Connor. Connor is 19, attends music school, and is unlikely to have an interest in any aspect of the business. Natalie is 22, and has always been interested in banking. She has completed a summer internship at a local bank and will graduate next year with a degree in finance.

Here's what Michael came up with as a personal vision after these in-depth discussions with his family.

> I will commit at least five more years to aggressively growing the business, even though there may be opportunities along the way to sell it to a large competitor who has twice expressed an interest in acquiring ABC.

> In five years, Joan and I expect to have a better idea regarding Natalie's possible interest in joining the family business someday.

> Both my parents and Joan's are alive and in reasonably good health, but Joan's parents live about 400 miles from us. There is, of course, the possibility that the failing health of a parent could cause a change in our plans, especially since neither Joan nor I have any siblings who can lend a hand in caring for an ailing parent.

Looking further down the road, Joan and I want to buy a house on a lake that is located closer to Joan's parents as a retreat for ourselves and our children, using it only occasionally at first, but more often as we grow older.

At the end of this personal vision exercise, Michael and Joan both realized how important it was for them to thoroughly discuss, on a regular basis, the many possible scenarios they might face over the next five years, some of which they had not previously considered. (For instance, Natalie might decide to abandon her plans to become a banker and to instead play a more active role in the family business at an earlier time than anyone expected.) As a result, Michael and Joan saved all of their notes from these discussions and made plans to go through the exercise every January to make absolutely certain that the vision for their personal lives was up-to-date so that it could be the basis of revaluating the vision for ABC Engineering.

In the sample plan for ABC Engineering you'll see a little bit later, you'll note that Michael's personal vision is not included as part of the strategic plan. This is not only because the personal vision of the leader is extremely personal and confidential but also because sharing it with others can potentially cause major issues. For example, if Michael's personal vision included his plans to sell the business within the next five years, revealing his intentions could cause havoc throughout his organization.

Excellence Best Practice: Creating the Organizational Vision, Mission, Values, and Beliefs

Leaders develop an organizational destination, craft a mission statement, and identify the supporting values and beliefs.

It's important that you next identify what and where you want your organization to be in the future, who needs your organization, and how your values and beliefs will fulfill your mission and vision.

Your corporate vision is a short statement that encapsulates what you want to be or where you want to go, and is the primary focus and end-point of planning. Without a vision, there is no need or point to planning.

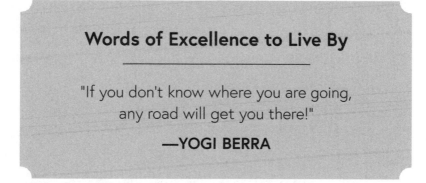

Words of Excellence to Live By

"If you don't know where you are going, any road will get you there!"

—YOGI BERRA

Please note that, even after you have created the vision statement for your organization, it can still change in the future. In fact, you'll see later in this chapter that, after having created your corporate vision statement, you will be objectively evaluating the external environment (the economy, competition, technology, and so on) as you go through the planning process. During that exercise, it is sometimes necessary to modify the vision for your organization, especially if you find there are environmental factors at work that will make your vision too difficult to achieve. Please keep this in mind as you create the first draft of your organizational vision.

There are two very important things to remember about organizational vision. First, it should be created by you, the leader, so that it is not at odds with your personal vision. You definitely want to be sure your employees will understand it, and they might even help you modify it slightly so that they can understand it, but it should still describe precisely where you want the organization to go. Second, while the organizational vision is often shared with customers and the public at large, it is actually intended for internal use since it should guide the behavior of your employees every day by describing exactly where your company is headed.

Excellence Process Insight

Your corporate vision must drive the behavior of your employees every day by providing them with a crystal-clear explanation of exactly where you want the company to go.

Corporate vision statements serve as an expectation. That's why they are usually written in the future tense, focusing on what the organization "will be" or "will become."

In his plan for ABC Engineering, Michael created the following corporate vision statement:

ABC Engineering will be the preferred source for water restoration services in Baltimore County.

It's important that you're able to determine when you've achieved your vision so be sure that it can somehow be measured. Since ABC Engineering wants to be the preferred source among Baltimore County contractors, Michael will be conducting an annual survey of contractors (including both current and potential customers), asking them to rank water restoration companies in order of their preference.

Although the end product is, by definition, quite brief, creating the corporate vision statement for your organization can be a challenging assignment. It's possible that you will need help from someone, but it's well worth the effort to achieve total clarity so that your employees know why they come to work every day. The organizational vision needs to be communicated to your employees over, and over, and over again.

The process of linking your corporate vision to your plan is similar to boarding a flight from New York to Atlanta. The captain has identified Atlanta as the specific destination (the vision). He and his crew have a crystal-clear understanding of both the destination and the plan to get there. Avionics, the control tower, and other factors may dictate that the plan be altered along the way to accommodate for weather or air traffic, but the destination is still Atlanta, and the pilot still has control systems in place to make sure everything is going as planned (altitude, fuel use, etc.). Likewise, in your business there will be environmental factors that may require you to alter your plan and control systems (budgets and dashboards) to monitor your progress.

By the way, vision statements and mission statements are often confused with one another. While vision is focused on the future (what you want your organization to become), mission statements are usually written in the present tense, describing exactly what your organization does, and for what audience or customer group. ABC Engineering's mission reads as follows:

> ABC Engineering consistently delivers the most complete range of safe and reliable water restoration solutions in Baltimore County.

Let's look next at organizational values and beliefs. These are operating principles that help employees and leaders do the right things and ensure the appropriate supporting behaviors are consistent throughout the organization. ABC's operating principles look like this:

- → We believe in treating our customers and each other with dignity and respect.
- → We believe in providing the greatest customer care in our industry.
- → We believe in sustaining a healthy environment in everything we do.

→ We believe that our success is driven by unsolicited referrals from our customers, who truly value our service.

→ We believe in protecting the health and well-being of our customers, employees, and the community at large.

→ We believe that our market leadership requires us to employ the most technically trained professionals, utilizing the most advanced equipment and techniques available.

Values and beliefs are observable to anyone who works with the company, including customers, vendors, and partners. They not only describe the culture of the organization, but they bring that culture to life. They can and should be used to disqualify applicants who don't share the stated values and beliefs and to evaluate whether current employees are acting in accordance with them. Most important of all, they must accurately describe how

Excellence Process Insight

A strong leader is a role model for exhibiting behaviors that are congruent with the organization's values and beliefs. In an organization of excellence, all leaders model the appropriate behavior; they do not tolerate behavior that is at odds with company values and beliefs. They know the stated values and beliefs become meaningless when they are not backed up by action.

you, the leader, actually conduct business most of the time. This is not to say that you never act outside of these standards, but that you do so very rarely, that you notice when you do go outside the lines, and that you acknowledge what has happened and course-correct quickly.

Excellence Best Practice: Analyzing the External Environment

Leaders identify the reality facing the organization.

Leaders of organizations of excellence acknowledge that growth and success are impossible unless they look objectively at the forces affecting current and future opportunities. They constantly identify and analyze the reality in which their organization operates. For the leader of an organization of excellence, the job of defining reality literally never stops.

Excellence Process Insight

Defining reality means taking a continuous, candid look at the current and future business environment.

Here's what Michael came up with as an analysis of the external environment facing ABC Engineering.

Key Environmental Factors (Positive and Negative) That Will Affect the Industry in the Next Three Years

The commercial building industry in Baltimore County will increase by 2%, 3%, and 2.5% over the next three years.

The cost of environmentally friendly chemicals will continue to rise faster than the rate of inflation.

As our competitors consolidate, price increases passed on to our customers will not exceed 1.5% per year.

Government regulations pertaining to environmentally friendly materials will continue to be a factor, but to a lesser extent than previously.

Attracting new engineers to our industry will continue to be a challenge.

The percentage of our employees who speak English will gradually decline.

Fuel prices will remain relatively stable over the next three years.

Leaders of organizations of excellence continuously gather and study the company's competitive landscape. This information is critical to their planning; often, the plan must be changed because the competitive landscape has changed. For instance, perhaps a competitor was bought out or went out of business, or a new competitor has entered the arena. The analysis can be as detailed or as simple as you want—but it must be a constant feature of your business because the competitive landscape does not stay the same for long.

Excellence Best Practice: Conducting a SWOT Analysis

Leaders start and support a team discussion by assessing the organization's strengths, weaknesses, opportunities, and threats.

You can further refine your analysis by assessing your strengths, weaknesses, opportunities, and threats. This is a way of internalizing the external environment, which you know you can't control, by identifying and minimizing the negative effects of any adverse external realities.

A SWOT analysis is a critical planning tool. It looks at the organization's known strengths, weaknesses, and opportunities, and also at the threats that can affect the company. You want to leverage strengths, prioritize opportunities, diminish weaknesses, and defend against threats.

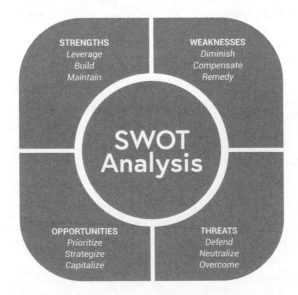

Excellence Process Insight

- Strengths are things you do well or perhaps better than anyone else—the things that set you apart from the competition.

- Weaknesses are areas where you need to improve or where a competitor is better.

- Opportunities are possibilities for growth and competitive advantage.

- Threats are adverse conditions you might face that are out of your control.

Business owners/leaders of organizations of excellence complete an in-depth SWOT analysis at least once per year and review it quarterly. New information may require a modification to the plan or may require that the plan be rewritten altogether.

Excellence Best Practice: Revisiting the Organizational Vision

Leaders reassess both the vision statement and the mission statement.

Based on what you have learned, you decide whether you need to make any changes to your organizational vision. If what you have learned about the reality within which your company is operating or about your strengths, weaknesses, opportunities, or threats leads you to believe your vision/mission is either too aggressive or not aggressive enough, you update it accordingly.

Excellence Best Practice: Identifying Key Priorities

Leaders set no more than three strategic priorities for the organization.

Several opportunities or threats will emerge from the work you've done thus far. Building on that work, identify the one, two, or three most critical priorities. These are known as key priorities.

The very first time you go through this planning process, most of the key priorities are likely to come from your list of weaknesses since it's difficult to take advantage of the opportunities until those obstacles are overcome. For instance, if high customer turnover is a major issue and you're not getting as much repeat business as you should from your current clients because they're experiencing quality problems, it's very likely that fixing that issue is going to be one of your key priorities. However, as your perpetual planning process is implemented and your organization moves forward, you may find yourself more and more able to focus your efforts on taking advantage of strategic opportunities since you'll

Excellence Process Insight

———————————————

Planning is a way of life, not a project.

reach a point where most weaknesses have already been addressed. (You can see now, I think, why it's absolutely critical to make sure the Excellence Process is repeated over time, as a way of doing business, day after day, quarter after quarter, year after year, and is never abandoned.)

There should be no more than three key priorities since any more are hard to address over the three- to- five-year planning period you are working on.

Excellence Best Practice: Establishing Clear Expectations for Each Key Priority

Leaders quantify measurable expectations in specific areas of strategic importance.

Once the top three priorities have been identified, set quantitative expectations for each of them. Quantifying these expectations allows you to regularly monitor progress towards achieving your key priorities. When you break expectations into measurable numerical goals, you create a clear target to aim for—and you make it easier for your team to hit that target.

This is a vitally important step. If you haven't figured out how you will know when you have completed and fulfilled a key priority, you might as well not have identified it at all. For example, if the key priority is "reduce customer turnover," you may want to set some specific expectations for 12, 24, and 36 months, measured by either "percentage of customers lost," or by a more positive measure, such as "percentage of customers retained." As an initial expectation, you might end up aiming for a 20% increase in the annual percentage of customers retained by the end of the current fiscal year, compared with the previous fiscal year.

The word "expectations" is important here. When setting these measures, you want to communicate to people that these truly are expected outcomes, not pie-in-the-sky goals or objectives. At the same time, you have to be sure to make the expectations realistic in terms of both quantity and timeframe. Having done that, make it clear that these are expectations with accountability for success attached to them. Keep in mind that meeting a realistic expectation should not bring a reward since that's what employees are already being paid to do. Rewards are earned only after expectations have been exceeded.

Excellence Best Practice: Setting Action Items, Due Dates, and Assignment of Responsibilities

Leaders decide what needs to be done, by whom, and by when.

You have a far better chance of achieving the key priorities you've identified if you assign specific action items with clear, attainable due dates to specific individuals in the company. Your people need to know exactly what they need to do to move forward on a key priority, who is ultimately accountable for doing it, and by when it needs to be done. If they don't have clarity on those issues, you can expect the action item to be unfulfilled or delayed. (A side note: Experience in multiple industries over five decades has shown us that due dates on action items are most realistic, and thus most likely to be met, when they are worked out collaboratively and not imposed upon team members without discussion.)

We strongly recommend using a tool known as RACI for clarifying accountabilities on your key priorities and their action items. RACI defines roles and responsibilities, streamlines effort, accelerates progress, facilitates task management, improves communication, and increases the likelihood of success.

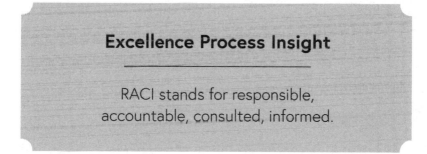

Excellence Process Insight

RACI stands for responsible, accountable, consulted, informed.

Here's how it works. All individuals participating in attaining the key priority are categorized by designations that clearly define their roles and responsibilities. These designations follow the RACI acronym, which is laid out below.

R: Responsible. The people who actually perform the activity, do the work, or manage the lead work group. These are typically people to whom action items are assigned.

→ Actively involved in implementing and managing one or more of the key priorities.

→ Part of the team developing action items for the key priorities delegated to them by the accountable individual.

→ Meets with assigned individuals to set due dates.

→ Holds the assigned individuals accountable for completing the action times by the due dates.

→ Sets dates and holds check-in meetings with assigned individuals to check progress on action items and make adjustments if needed.

→ Ensures the assigned individuals have the necessary support and resources to complete action items.

→ Gives status updates to the accountable individual on the progress of the key priorities and the action items.

→ Examples: Vice president of sales/operations, manager of a department.

A: Accountable. The one person with the ultimate ownership of the key priority. This is the primary decision maker, the person with the most authority on this key priority, and the person held responsible for its fulfillment.

→ Ultimately accountable for the achievement of one or more key priorities.

→ Delegates to the responsible individual to implement and manage the action items for the key priority.

→ Can be part of the team developing the action items.

→ Can only be one individual and must not be the responsible individual.

→ Can be an individual outside the company or an advisory board member.

→ May bring in consulted individuals.

→ Responsible for the communication plan.

→ Examples: Business owner, EVP, CFO, COO.

C: Consulted. People who are involved in discussions regarding developments in the key priority and whose feedback is expected as a result. They offer advice and insights along the way.

→ Can be involved in the planning, implementation, and managing of key priorities or action items as a resource.

→ Possess expertise related to the key priority or action items.

→ Part of the team developing action items.

→ May be an outside resource.

→ Can slow down or even stop a project based on their expertise.

→ Examples: Marketing/operations consultant, CPA, board of directors.

I: Informed. People who are kept up-to-date on developments of the key priority and whose feedback is welcomed but not required. These are individuals who are "in the loop."

→ Has no involvement in managing or implementing the key priorities or action items.

→ Receives updates about the progress of the key priority.

→ Can offer feedback.

→ Examples: Non-managers, other department heads, entire company.

Notice there can be several responsible for each key priority, several consulted per key priority and action item, and many informed throughout the process, but only one accountable individual per key priority.*

The accountable individual accepts personal responsibility for the achievement of the key priority. If something goes wrong, the accountable individual is at fault, no matter what—like the captain of a ship. This is why it is so very important to choose the right individual and to ensure that you have the time and ability to fill that role if it ends up being you.

The RACI system creates teamwork and synergy within the company and continued momentum to achieve results. With this framework in place to minimize confusion and provide mission clarity, your team members can focus their efforts effectively on achieving the key priority.

Excellence Best Practice: Allocating Resources to Accomplish Action Plans

Leaders ensure that the accountable person for each key priority has the resources available to be able to accomplish the action items and create the appropriate budgets.

It is important that you set aside the necessary funds so that those who are tasked with specific action items will have the needed financial and personnel resources. Action items must be resourced as part of the overall company budgeting process. The resources

---

* As a general rule, RACI should be used for the entire key priority, not for individual action items. However, RACI is a flexible tool, and your organization may reach a point where it is large enough to create a RACI group devoted to a single action item.

may be allocated to the key priority as a whole and then divided among the action items. The accountable individual is responsible for getting the approval or approving the resources.

Typically, the accountable individual manages the budget for each key priority, and the responsible individual manages the budget for the individual action items. Resources must be first allocated to Key Priority 1, then to Key Priority 2, and then to Key Priority 3.

Excellence Best Practice: Conducting Regular Planning Reviews

Leaders evaluate progress and course-correct as necessary.

Like pilots who constantly monitor their course, you must constantly monitor the progress of your plans. When the plan is documented and reviewed against a checklist regularly, the odds of success increase.

It is your responsibility as the leader to relentlessly drive the review process. This process requires rigor and discipline and can be conducted by outside resources if you wish.

Review meetings are separate meetings, typically held every three months, and are not a part of regular team or project meetings. They need to be pre-scheduled at the beginning of the year; management attendance should be mandatory.

Again, if there is no follow up to the plan, no assumption that the plan is going to need course correction along the way, and no effort to make that course correction, then all the work you have done thus far is just a binder sitting on a bookshelf.

Excellence Process Insight

There is no point in spending time planning if there is no way to measure success and adjust your approach.

A Sample Strategic Plan

Planning is the foundation of the Excellence Process, and it takes up a significant amount of the leader's time, energy, and attention. I've given you a lot to consider in this chapter, and I realize it all may seem overwhelming. To help you become more comfortable with everything we've discussed, I'm including a sample plan, reflecting all the steps carried out by the leader of our fictional company, ABC Engineering. Please take a close look at this plan before you move on to the second P (Positions), and feel free to come back to it as necessary as you make your way through the book.

Sample Strategic Plan: ABC Engineering, Inc.

Our Vision

→ ABC Engineering will be the preferred source for water restoration services in Baltimore County.

Our Mission

→ ABC Engineering consistently delivers the most complete range of safe and reliable water restoration solutions in Baltimore County.

Values and Beliefs

→ We believe in treating our customers and each other with integrity and respect.

→ We believe in providing the greatest customer care available in our industry.

→ We believe in sustaining a healthy environment in everything we do.

→ We believe that our success is driven by unsolicited referrals from our customers who truly value our service.

→ We believe in protecting the health and well-being of our customers, employees, and the community at large.

→ We believe that our market leadership requires us to employ the most technically trained professionals, utilizing the most advanced equipment and techniques available.

Key Environmental Factors (Positive and Negative) That Will Affect the Industry in the Next Three Years

→ The commercial building industry in Baltimore County is expected to grow by 2%, 3%, and 2.5% over the next three years.

→ The cost of chemicals used in our industry will continue to rise faster than the general inflation rate.

→ As our competitors consolidate, industry price increases to our customers will not exceed 1.5% per year.

→ Government regulations pertaining to environmentally friendly materials will continue to be a factor, but to a lesser extent than previously.

→ Attracting new engineers to our industry will continue to be a challenge.

→ The percentage of our employees who speak English will gradually decline.

→ Fuel prices will remain relatively stable over the next three years.

Three Greatest Strengths

→ Highly trained technicians with the most advanced equipment available.

→ Fastest response time in the industry.

→ High customer referral rate due to the quality of our work.

Three Greatest Weaknesses

→ Failure to effectively market and promote our reputation as the leader in quality.

→ Staffing to keep pace with our growth.

→ Age and condition of our field equipment.

Three Greatest Opportunities

→ Expand water restoration services to one or more neighboring counties.

→ Begin providing lawn chemical applications to current water restoration companies.

→ Take on commercial water engineering customers in our current market area of Baltimore County.

Three Greatest Threats

→ Slow-down in construction market due to changes in zoning or interest rates.

→ Change in political climate could result in more regulations governing our industry.

→ Two of our local competitors are considering merging.

Key Priorities

→ Priority 1: Promoting Our Reputation for Quality

- Responsible: Carol
- Accountable: Michael
- Consulted: Fran (outside consultant)
- Informed: Entire company

Expectations

Key Measures of Success	Current Year	Year 1 of Plan	Year 2 of Plan	Year 3 of Plan
Total Number of New Customers	30%	38%	48%	62%
Number of New Customers from Referrals	15%	21%	29%	40%
Percent of Customers Retained	70%	74%	80%	87%
Percent Increase in Website Leads	N.A.	28%	43%	58%

*Action Steps | Assigned to Be Completed by*_____

Hire contractor to evaluate website and social media effectiveness.	Vera	10/31, Year 1
Create lead-tracking process and dashboard for tracking those leads.	Vera	10/31, Year 1
Collect customer testimonials and post to website.	Vera	3/31, Year 1
Develop strategy for generating more testimonials and leads.	Jack	6/30, Year 1
Create incentive compensation plan to generate referrals.	Jack	1/31, Year 2
Develop incentive compensation plan to reward customer retention.	Jack	1/31, Year 3

→ Priority 2: Develop Incentive Compensation Plan to Reward Customer Retention

- Responsible: Juan
- Accountable: Michael
- Consulted: Fran (outside consultant)
- Informed: Entire company

Expectations

Key Measures of Success	Current Year	Year 1 of Plan	Year 2 of Plan	Year 3 of Plan
% of Jobs Filled within 14 days	68%	70%	74%	80%
% of Employees with ABC Certification	0%	55%	65%	75%
% of Employees Leaving within 120 days	18%	16%	13%	10%
% of Employees Staying Longer than 1 year	64%	69%	74%	80%

*Action Steps | Assigned to Be Completed by*_____

Action Steps	Assigned to	Be Completed by
Develop job description for new Human Resources Manager.	Michael	2/28, Year 1
Hire new Human Resources Manager.	Michael	6/30, Year 1
Find or develop assessment screening test for recruiting new employees.	HR Mgr	8/31, Year 1
Create recruiting system and design onboarding program for new hires.	HR Mgr	1/31, Year 2
Implement equipment maintenance program to improve employee productivity.	Tina	5/31, Year 2
Design and implement exit interview program.	HR Mgr	1/31, Year 3

18

Positions

So far, you have created a plan. You've set the vision, the mission, and the driving values and beliefs; you've conducted a thorough analysis of the external factors affecting the organization; you've decided on the top three key priorities; and you've developed action items to achieve them. You now have the *what* (the plan, mission, vision, and the associated accountabilities). What's next?

Now it's time to determine the *how* (meaning the way you are going to execute the plan) and the *who* (meaning who is going to do what). Specifically, you will focus on whether you can fulfill your vision with the current structure. If the company is not yet structured correctly, you will focus on what kind of people you need.

Your organization deserves a streamlined, consciously designed organizational structure, one that minimizes overlap of functions within each position and gives you the capacity to perform at a high level and adapt to change quickly, so you are positioned to adapt to the realities of your marketplace. You will begin with the big picture, identifying the perfect structure needed to achieve the organizational vision you've identified, and move forward from there.

Here are the positions best practices we'll examine in this chapter.

→ Determining the organizational structure.

→ Identifying skill sets and other attributes needed for each function.

→ Creating or updating job descriptions for each function.

Excellence Best Practice: Determining the Organizational Structure

Leaders create an organizational chart that defines the major functions, reporting structure, roles, and responsibilities for each contributor in the organization.

You will now begin to create an all-new organizational chart, one that defines the major functions required. These are the functions without which implementation of the plan would be impossible.

Leaders of organizations of excellence realize that they cannot achieve the vision on their own. They know they need the efforts of others to bring the strategic initiatives they've identified to fulfillment. So they take the time to figure out what organizational structure is needed for the future.

Remember: You are starting with a clean slate. Assume you have no current organizational chart and no employees.

Excellence Process Insight

Leaders of organizations of excellence look beyond their current structure and determine what structural changes are needed for the future. They determine the major functions that will be essential to success and then decide on the required roles, responsibilities, and reporting relationships for all the functions within the company.

This is an essential part of the process that will point you toward a brand new organizational chart based on implementing your plan to achieve the new organizational vision. Start with the end in mind. What will it take to create happy customers or clients? What are the major functions that will be required to create and deliver your product or service within your various market segments?

Start with what you will require from your executive team members, the main individuals engaged in the planning and achievement of the organizational vision. Bear in mind that these "inner circle" people can be employees who report to you, or they can be professionals from outside the company, such as a CPA, an attorney, or a consultant. They deserve a spot on the new organizational chart either way.

Begin by creating a visual breakdown that shows your current organizational chart (even if you have never put one together before). There is special software you can use to do this, but you can also use PowerPoint. If you have a human resources group, they can point you toward the tools you need. Whatever method you choose to use, start with the top-tier jobs—you and the people who report directly to you. The evaluation you're about to perform can be repeated later for the remainder of the positions in your organization, but you must first focus on those at the top.

List only the major function for each position in your inner circle, not the title or the name of the person currently holding that position. (It's important to avoid names so you can maintain objectivity.)

It's likely you'll come up with something like this:

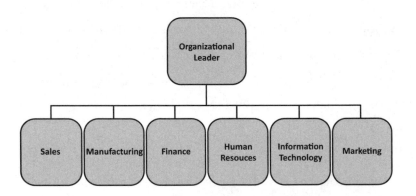

You've just created a visual picture of where you are now organizationally. Now it's time to take a close look at your new strategic plan, so you can determine what structure will be necessary to achieve it. Things may or may not need to change, but only you can decide that.

For instance, let's assume that you manufacture and sell consumer items—party goods, let's say—and you have recently decided that only a portion of your product line will continue to be made in your domestic manufacturing facilities. The other portion will be purchased from a variety of new suppliers from around the globe. This is a major change, but necessary if your company is to remain competitive. In addition, your strategic plan calls for selling to customers in a few selected countries rather than restricting yourself to the United States. These significant changes need to be reflected in your new organizational chart, which might look like the one below:

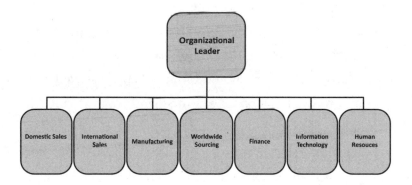

This second organizational chart reflects where you're going as a company. Eventually, you will proceed through the rest of the chart with this same approach, identifying only functions and not names. But save that step until you've completed the positions best practices for your inner circle.

Understand that there are certain basic ground rules you must follow in setting up the new organizational chart. No employee should have more than one boss, and there must be no overlap between roles and certainly no duplication. You'll also want to make sure there is a succession plan for all key positions, including yours, so that your company isn't vulnerable to the possibility of a crucial employee leaving without warning, intentionally or otherwise.

When I first did this exercise for our company, I added three new senior positions—two because of where we were going as an organization and the third because one function on the organizational chart had too many direct reports (it wasn't practical to assume a single individual could manage the whole portfolio). When I shared the first draft of this new organizational structure with my team, I found some interesting, and predictable, reactions. There were lots of questions and suggestions as to how the new organizational chart should look. When we started assigning names to the functions, I saw firsthand what a "land grab" looks like, as people tried to assume personal control of more of the chart than they'd been assigned. That's natural when you're dealing with high performers. There were strong emotions and some initial hurt feelings—but fortunately, we were able to come together as a group, focus on the future we were creating, and look for ways to make the new organizational structure work.

Excellence Best Practice: Identifying Skill Sets and Other Attributes Needed for Each Function

Without using any names of actual employees, leaders identify the skills, experience, attitude, results, cognitive skills, and habits required for each function.

Here I have to emphasize the vital importance of doing your best to forget about every employee who is already part of the organization. The fact that you know the name of someone in your inner circle, or anywhere else, is irrelevant to this best practice. Yes, you know their strengths and weaknesses, but leave the names out of your evaluations until later. Only after you've completed those evaluations should you look at your "inventory" of people who already work for the organization.

Using the future-focused organizational structure you've created, your job now is to record the following information for each function:

→ The primary duties and responsibilities of each position (list only a few key items).
→ Your best understanding of the profile of the ideal candidate to fill each position. (This should be your "wish list" of education, experience, and so on.)

A tool we call the SEARCH model is helpful in identifying the specific criteria used to evaluate both current and future employees. Once you have filled in all the SEARCH blanks, you will be able to further define the elements as: non-negotiables, should haves, and nice-to-haves.

SKILLS	EXPERIENCE	ATTITUDE	RESULTS	COGNITIVE SKILLS	HABITS
Specific abilities required by the position	Done this type of job, assumed the responsibility, and applied the knowledge required by position	State of mind of the candidate and self-confidence	Accomplishments that verify one's ability	Ability to learn/process information required by the job	Specific behaviors and actions required of the job or not desired in the company culture

Ideally, you should only be focused on the top-tier positions at this point. This same evaluation can be done later with the remaining jobs, many of which will have also changed due to the new strategic plan.

It's important to note here that you yourself need to periodically monitor whether you are still qualified to lead the organization forward. This is a sensitive topic, but it's one that must be addressed. Being the leader does not necessarily qualify you to lead the organization indefinitely. One of the best methods of determining whether your own leadership skills still qualify you to run the organization is to rely on an outside board for their candid input as your company grows. More will be said about outside boards in Chapter 21, but it's important to mention them here because your organizational plan should include outside advisors who provide skill sets that your business needs—and insights on critical questions like this one.

Excellence Best Practice: Creating or Updating Job Descriptions for Each Function

Leaders define the specific requirements needed for the successful completion of the job functions and responsibilities.

Again, you will complete this best practice for your own inner circle first, and avoid the use of any names.

Here is a sample SEARCH summary for ABC Engineering's finance director.

Skills

→ Ability to create, analyze, and report accurate financial information to the leader.

→ Ability to negotiate large contracts and minimize risk to the company.

Experience

→ Minimum of ten years in a financial capacity at mid-sized business.

→ Minimum of two years in a management position.

Attitude

→ Accepts and acts within our organization's core values.

Results

→ Achieved less than 1% in bad debt in each year.

→ Produced complete financial statements including all necessary supporting documentation.

Cognitive Skills

→ Can use several popular accounting software programs.

→ Attention to detail.

Habits

→ Follows processes without exception.

→ Maintains an organized and clean workspace.

And here is a condensed sample job description for the same position.

Job Title: Finance Director

Date Created/Updated: 10/25

Reports To: President

Department/Division: Finance

Number of Employees Supervised: 3

Salary Range: $90,000–$100,000

Job Description: Accountable for all aspects of the finance department, including the primary functions of accounting, payroll, accounts payable, accounts receivable, and bookkeeping.

Essential Duties and Responsibilities: Track expenses and identify variances, assist in negotiating contracts, assist outside CPA in preparing financial statements, and manage bad debt. Provide guidance on maximizing profit and cutting waste.

Required Skills:

→ Ability to create, analyze, and report accurate financial information to owners/leaders.

→ Ability to negotiate large contracts and minimize risk to the company.

→ Communicate with customers and leadership.

Required Experience:

→ Minimum of ten years in a financial capacity at mid-sized business.

→ Minimum of two years in a management position.

Required Attitude:

→ [Use your core values.]

Required Results:

→ Achieves less than 1% in bad debt in any year.

→ Produces complete financial statements including all necessary supporting documentation within a week of close.

→ Saves employer money in the negotiation process.

Required Cognitive Abilities:

→ Critical thinker.

→ Attention to detail.

Required Habits:

→ Follows processes without exception.

→ Maintains an organized and clean workspace.

Success Looks Like:

→ Success in this position requires the individual to develop and follow a process that is consistent, predictable, and reliable.

→ Manage and coach three employees, including developing a transition plan for bookkeeper who is retiring next year.

→ Attend monthly mandatory planning meetings with specific key priorities:

- Evaluate and train dealers on financial reporting systems.
- Look at the company proposals to validate our pricing model and finance assumptions.
- The role this individual will play is as a consultant on these priorities, as these are major investments for the company. The plan in the future is to bring on a CFO; evaluation will be made after top three key priorities are achieved to determine fit.

→ This person will be required to present monthly to the leadership team the following reports:

- Accounts payable/receivable.
- Projected revenue (forecast three to six months).
- Financial statements of current and prior year comparison of the balance sheet, income statement, and cash flow statement.
- Wage report.

- Detailed list of all expenses.
- Forecasted cash for 90 days, six months, and one year.

Once you have created the relevant job descriptions (or gotten outside help in doing so, which is fine), you face a number of important questions. Do you have the right people on board to fulfill each role? Is each employee in a position to know and agree to the expectations of the role required in the function?

We'll look more closely at those issues in the next chapter.

Excellence Process Insight

Once you have defined the major functions, you can decide on the required roles and responsibilities. Once you know the roles and responsibilities, you can identify the skill sets required to effectively do the job required of the function. With all this information on structure and positions, you can create accurate, robust job descriptions for each function within your organization.

As you proceed through these three best practices, remember the final destination: to achieve the vision and implement the plan.

19

People

People are your strongest asset—or your greatest weakness. Your organization is only as strong as its weakest employee. By continually training and developing your employees, you can dramatically increase your chances of future success. Consider training and development to be an ongoing commitment—not the first thing that gets cut when there are challenges.

Once all the job profiles and job descriptions of each function have been completed in the second P (Positions), you should have a sense of what the right person looks like for each role. Now you need to determine whether this person already exists within your company. If not, you are ready to search for the person with the specific skill sets required. Following a diligent process, you can go about selecting the very best people for each function.

Your single biggest challenge as a leader lies in finding and keeping the people who present the right fit with the company's functions and culture. This is a critical responsibility, one that takes time and effort to fulfill. Finding and holding on to a "best fit" employee for every function on the organizational chart is not an overnight process.

Recruiting, hiring, and developing employees is a major investment in time, attention, and resources. However, every leader of an organization of excellence with whom I've had the privilege of working has concluded that this investment to find and retain the right people is far more efficient than hiring quickly to fill a vacant slot with a "warm body." Remember, the cost of making the wrong hire can be, and usually is, enormous in terms of time, money, and lost opportunities for growth.

Achieving excellence for your organization depends on securing and holding onto the right people. As the leader, you are responsible for making sure that happens. By following the best practices outlined below, you can stay objective and focused on the plan as you make what are bound to be some difficult choices.

Here are the people best practices we'll examine in this chapter.

→ Assessing current employees to see who fits and who doesn't.
→ Establishing a budget for training and development.
→ Creating individual development plans for each employee.
→ Determining new employees needed and recruiting.

Excellence Best Practice: Assessing Current Employees to See Who Fits and Who Doesn't

Without getting emotionally involved, leaders decide who, from the current team, is best able to fill the functions required to achieve the organizational vision.

Some current employees will fit well where they are; some will fit better in a different role from what they do now; and some may not fit at all into the new structure. Stay objective as you make these decisions. (You may need help from an outside source, such as a consultant, as you carry out this assessment.)

Questions to ask yourself as you implement this difficult best practice include:

→ Which current employees will fit in immediately with the strategic plan?

→ Which current employees might fit in with the strategic plan with some development?

→ Can you provide training/support to people so they can do the job?

→ Which current employees will not fit in as the organization changes to accomplish the plan?

→ Are you being emotionally influenced by your history with certain employees?

Excellence Best Practice: Establishing a Budget for Training and Development

Leaders of organizations of excellence set aside budgets every year for the development of their people.

Allocating the time and money to develop your people sends a strong, positive message to your employees that you care about them. Remember, you are developing more than just skills.

Attitudes and behavior play a major role in the ultimate success of your people.

Before deciding who needs what training and reinforcement, you should have a budget already established from which the funds for training and reinforcement will be readily available. If the budget is not already established and available, there could be a tendency to postpone individual development until the money becomes available. That's a mistake that will keep your organization from attaining excellence.

Questions to ask yourself as you implement this best practice include:

→ What is your formal training and development plan?

→ Do you provide equal availability and opportunity for growth and development to all employees, regardless of their position in the organization?

A classic blind spot in this area, as you'll recall, is to devote attention and resources to the development of front-line employees but not to managers (and yourself). Don't fall into that trap. Doing so will drive your organization into at-risk territory.

Excellence Best Practice: Creating Individual Development Plans for Each Employee

Leaders make sure employees are continually assessed to determine what will help them improve their performance.

This best practice is vitally important if you wish to develop and retain the right people. Communicate with your employees and agree to an active, collaborative plan for individual growth and development.

Questions to ask yourself as you implement this best practice include:

→ Are you doing all you can to assure your people get the training and development they need to perform their job now?

→ Are you doing all you can to help your people develop their career path within your organization?

→ What process are you using to assess the team's training needs? (See Chapter 21, "Performetrics.")

→ If there is no process in place, who can you work with to create and sustain one?

Excellence Best Practice: Determining New Employees Needed and Recruiting

Leaders launch an ongoing recruitment process.

Once you have determined which of your employees provide the right fit for your company's various functions, you will find that some functions remain vacant. This means recruiting from outside of your organization to fill these functions.

An effective recruiting process includes multiple interviews and some sort of assessment test to determine fit. If you do not have a strong process for effectively recruiting, screening, interviewing, and testing prospective employees, you will want to get help from an expert to create a process you can administer yourself.

Excellence Process Insight

Recruiting is a way of life for organizations of excellence, not a one-time event.

There is no one recruitment process that's right for every organization, but here's something that applies to every leader reading this book: Organizations of excellence recruit with culture in mind so that every new employee has not just the skills and results, but the attitude and value system that fit. Be sure any new hire you seriously consider will fit your culture and present the right daily attitude about working for your company. David Sandler used to warn me about people who claimed to be looking for a long-term career but were really aiming to "quit at 45 and retire at 65." This is another way of saying that you're looking, not just for the right resume and the right answers to the questions, but the right people—those who will contribute to your company because doing so is part of their personal mission. Your goal should be to hire only purpose-driven people into your organization.

Pre-employment assessments, conducted with the help of an outside partner, can be extremely helpful on this score and can also give you invaluable insights about a candidate's aptitudes and capacities. Use them!

The single best way to build the right team is to make fewer bad hires. It's for this reason that I've included, as an appendix, a comprehensive case study that shows just how important hiring and recruiting is to building an organization of excellence, and what some of the most dangerous mistakes are. You'll find it on page 185.

You'll find it on page 185.

Excellence Process Insight

The single best and most cost-effective way to build an excellent team is to avoid mistakes in hiring and recruiting.

You've already done a lot of the work necessary to create a successful recruiting and hiring process—what we call a hiring template. You should be able to look at your completed job description and know exactly what you are seeking in a candidate. Strive for a perfect match with your SEARCH criteria.

Use the hiring funnel below as a guideline for hiring the best person, making sure to conduct interviews with multiple people from the hiring side whenever possible. Don't rely on your own impressions too heavily. Be sure to get input and suggestions from other interviewers.

RECRUITING —— • Job Description   • SEARCH
• The Hiring Template • People Bank

INTERVIEWING —— • Preparation • Close
• Beginning • Debrief
• Middle

INVENTORYING —— • Personality • Specific Skills
• Skills/Attitudes

ASSESSMENT —— • Levels of Confidence
& DECISION
MAKING

HIRE!

Questions to ask yourself as you implement this best practice include:

→ Does your company take the time to find the "best fit" candidate, or are you just in a hurry to fill the position?

→ Do you match the applicant to the SEARCH criteria referenced in the job description?

→ How much does a bad hire really cost your company?

20

Processes

Afer the planning is in place, the positions are determined, and the right people are in the organization, great processes are the next signpost on the road to excellence.

A process is a series of actions you take in order to achieve a desired outcome. There are two key things to note here. First, we are talking about a series of actions carried out in a particular order; and second, the actions should result in the achievement of a desired outcome, one that has already been determined.

Organizations of excellence create and follow processes in every area of the company, for every function, without exception. These processes drive the various functions of the organization, but they are continually reviewed and upgraded to make sure they fit the plan and vision of the company.

This means employee input is essential. Average employees can follow good processes, but only strong employees will recognize when processes are no longer effective or know how to change them. This is one reason it is so important to identify the right people before attempting to identify the right processes.

Notice that there is one and only one best practice to follow here. Fulfilling it will require brutal honesty, a significant investment of time, and plenty of input from others in your organization.

Here is the processes best practice we'll examine in this chapter.

→ Evaluating and revising processes.

Insight of Excellence

Following a process doesn't mean being robotic or pretending you've suddenly acquired an engineering degree. It means acknowledging people should be attacking similar tasks in a similar way. For example: If you are effective at teaching your kids the best ways for them to stay on top of their monthly bill payments, and you then coach them well on what they've learned from you about carrying out the various steps, they will probably end up following the same process you follow. It works this way in business as well. You share a process that's proven effective: "When doing X, here is what we do."

Excellence Best Practice: Evaluating and Revising Processes

Leaders refer to the vision and the plan for the organization, evaluate the effectiveness of the current processes, and make any necessary improvements.

It is ultimately your responsibility as leader to confirm that there is, within each process, a series of steps that lead each function to the desired outcome you determined in planning. You must also identify other areas of the organization that would benefit from good processes and make sure those processes are created and followed. These, of course, are the "playbooks" I spoke about in Part One of this book. Playbooks come in all different shapes and sizes, depending on what they're trying to accomplish. A playbook can show an individual the steps for success, or it can show a team the steps necessary for success. Whether the objective is simple or complex, team-driven or individual-driven, long-term or short-term, if it is part of your plan, it needs a playbook—a process.

The Ten Key Attributes of an Excellent Process

1. Aligned with, and driven by, the plan.

2. Well-documented.

3. Clear, with no room for misinterpretation.

4. Repeatable.

5. People can and do commit to following it to the letter, with no exceptions.

6. Continuously re-evaluated to ensure ongoing effectiveness.

7. Job descriptions are linked to it.

8. Incentive compensation is linked to it, when appropriate.

9. Employee training and development are built around it.

10. Connected to someone who is accountable.

I realize that making all the above happen for every process in the organization may seem at first like an impossible task. Yet in companies of excellence, this fourth P is actually a logical outcome of the first three P's: a perpetual planning process, the right positions (structure), and people who are purpose-driven. Notice that a perpetual planning process results in a detailed to-do list for each and every employee in the organization, all tied to the expected outcomes specified in the plan. As we've already seen, the structure needed and people skills required to implement that plan include clear expectations for each job (as defined in the job description). With all of these things already in place, determining the necessary processes is simply the fulfillment of what has gone before. It's only "extra work" if you skip the first three P's.

Words of Excellence to Live By

"94% of problems in business are systems-driven. Only 6% are people-driven."

—W. EDWARDS DEMING

Questions to ask yourself as you implement this best practice include:

→ Does everyone have a playbook?

→ Is someone in the organization fully responsible for making certain that all ten key attributes of a good process are being met by all of your organization's playbooks?

→ Are you looking at your current processes objectively—or finding reasons not to invest the time, money, and other resources to document processes or make changes to improve them?

→ Which one new process (or update of an existing process) will have the biggest positive impact on your organization?

→ When will that work begin?

→ What are your plans for addressing the opportunities and challenges that will go along with implementing (or updating) this process?

21

Performetrics

Accountability for delivering outcomes that support the plan needs to connect to every individual in the company. Performetrics, the fifth P, is what makes that happen.

Performetrics focuses on the age-old saying: "If you can't measure it, you can't manage it." Once the planning is completed and is being executed through the essential positions in the organizational chart, once the people are in place to implement the plan, once effective processes have been established, progress must be measured through performance metrics—or performetrics.

These are more than just the typical company measures such as budget, income statement, balance sheet, and other financial reports. In organizations of excellence, the performetrics approach includes metrics for every employee on an individual basis. Performetrics measures are not just activities and behaviors; they connect to the outcomes of those activities and behaviors. If employees follow the processes, they will by definition be doing the activities and behaviors to achieve the desired outcomes that support your plan.

There are five best practices that organizations of excellence follow to create the very best performetrics. It's your job to make sure your organization implements all five.

Here are the performetrics best practices we'll examine in this chapter.

→ Establishing individual metrics for each employee.

→ Conducting regular performance appraisals/evaluations.

→ Conducting employee surveys.

→ Creating tracking reports to maintain control of the business.

→ Monitoring board/advisory group performance.

Excellence Best Practice: Establishing Individual Metrics for Each Employee

Leaders make sure measurable, individual benchmarks are in place for every employee.

Excellence Process Insight

You must set your own measurable performance benchmarks and find a way to hold yourself accountable for attaining them. Not doing so is a major blind spot.

This is one of the most effective ways of introducing accountability into an organization. The "Performetrics Revolution" must begin at the top level.

Leaders often say they want their employees to be more accountable but that they don't have time to create a complicated tracking system. Employees often say they would like to be more

Key Attributes of Effective Performetrics

→ Tied to the overall vision of the organization.

→ Tied to the top three key priorities.

→ Established for every function in the organization.

→ Documented in job descriptions and individual development and training plans.

→ Determine training needs of the company and individual employees.

→ Tied to compensation, specifically incentive-based functions.

→ Major part of employees' coaching sessions.

→ Competencies needed for achieving performetrics are required elements of the recruiting process.

→ You must have a process in place—a playbook—for achieving the desired outcome.

empowered. Setting up effective performetrics for individual employees addresses all three concerns. They make employees feel more empowered, while at the same time making them more accountable. The time it takes to set the program up is an excellent investment.

Here's how it works. Prior to any formal performance evaluation, employees need to collaboratively develop with a manager their performetrics agreement. Some of our clients ask that people sign these agreements, which is fine; others send an email reflecting the agreement that's been worked out and ask that the employee reply. Either approach works. The underlying principle remains the same: An agreement is negotiated and formally agreed to. This should be non-negotiable for every employee—including you! (Yes, that means you'll need to find someone with whom to develop your own performetrics agreement.)

This approach ensures that each employee, from the top down, knows exactly what is expected. The performetrics system provides the initial baseline from which to judge all performance.

Here's how it works. The employee and supervisor take the time to identify quantitative performance standards for the upcoming agreed-upon time period. I want to emphasize again that these standards must be negotiated, not dictated, since employees are agreeing that they will meet or exceed the standards that have been established.

Important: The standards that arise from these discussions are not "stretch goals." They are the expected level of performance. Only when performance exceeds the standard is it considered to be beyond expectations.

Excellence Process Insight

A real performetrics agreement is always the result of a collaborative discussion between two people. Only tasks and duties that are measurable and completely under the control of the employee should be included in this agreement.

Depending upon the level of the position in the organization, there could be as few as one measurable standard for the employee to focus on, or as many as five or six. In general, the lower the employee's position in the organization, the fewer standards there will be, since there will likely be very few duties over which the employee has total control at the lower levels.

Here are some sample metrics that are used in a performetrics agreement. Some are quite typical, and others are not. It's not an exhaustive list, but it will give you an idea of the kind of metrics you're looking for.

- → Average amount per sales transaction
- → Percent of sales generated by new products
- → Percent of sales generated by new customers
- → Number of new leads generated
- → Percent of leads converted to actual sales
- → Percent of quotes converted to actual sales

→ Number of error-free products/tasks

→ Percent of positions filled from inside candidates

→ Percent of employees who hold certain certifications

→ Percent of products delivered on time

→ Percent of deliveries made with no errors

→ Percent of orders filled completely

→ Invoice accuracy

Here is an example of a completed performetrics agreement from our fictional company, ABC Engineering:

Performetrics Agreement				
Job Title: Billing Clerk		Current Employee: Sally Sample		
Time Period Covered: 10/1–12/31	Today's Date: 9/28	Name of Supervisor: Betty Boss		
Duties for Which Employee Is Totally Responsible:	Method of Measurement:	Expected Outcome:	Actual Outcome:	% Over (+) % Under (-)
Prepare Customer Invoices Daily	Actual number of invoices prepared per day	50 per day		
Prepare Monthly Customer Statements	Actual number of customer statements prepared per month	Average should be 6/day or 120/month		

Prepare Credit Memos as Needed	Number of credit memos prepared	100% of credit memos prepared on time		
Enter Invoices into Computer System	Actual number of invoices entered into computer system	50 per day		

We agree on the duties for which the employee is responsible, the method of measurement, and the expected outcomes above.

Questions to ask yourself as you implement this best practice include:

→ What should you be tracking and holding people accountable for accomplishing?

→ How can you build a performetrics approach into specific jobs at your organization?

→ For which performetrics should you be holding yourself accountable to accomplish?

Excellence Best Practice: Conducting Regular Performance Appraisals/ Evaluations

Leaders ensure that each job description is up-to-date so that both the manager and the employee know the current expectations for the position.

Managers should utilize a closed-loop feedback process when evaluating performetrics. This evaluation is a never-ending process during the lifecycle of an employee. However, monitoring and tracking this information about progress is only one half of the loop. Analyzing the data and providing the employee with relevant feedback is the other half.

Once the performetrics agreements have been agreed to, goals have been established, quotas set, and action plans developed, this ongoing process of closed-loop feedback permits a manager to monitor and assess the employee's progress and provide a framework for constructive feedback and continuous improvement.

Excellence Process Insight

Thanks to the performetrics system, the performance evaluation becomes a simple matter of confirming whether numerical expectations are being met.

Through the closed-loop feedback process, the employee and manager operate as a self-regulating entity, working together to accomplish goals within a predetermined time frame. At our company, we ask the employee to track the metrics we've chosen during the performetrics discussion. That makes sense because we want the employee to be looking at these metrics often. It's the employee's responsibility to bring the metrics to each meeting with the manager. If the employee is on track, the manager gives positive feedback to reinforce the good behavior. If the employee gets off track, the manager can help by first calling attention to the off-course behavior or results, and then helping the employee to get back on track.

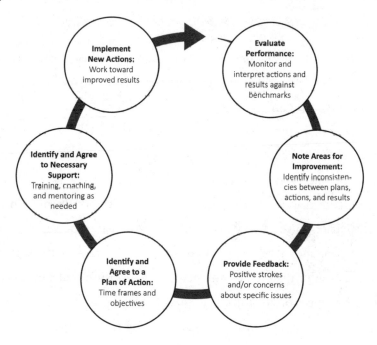

Questions to ask yourself as you implement this best practice include:

→ Are your job descriptions up-to-date, so that each employee knows the current expectations for the position?

→ Are your performetrics agreements current?

→ Are the primary duties and responsibilities from the current job description listed on the performance appraisal form so that the employee and manager are judging performance based on the same expectations?

Excellence Best Practice: Conducting Employee Surveys

Leaders of organizations of excellence know that employees will feel listened to and included when their input is sought and, when appropriate, acted upon.

Organizations of excellence get important insights on how they can improve by conducting comprehensive employee surveys at least every two years. (Once each year is better.)

Know that employees will be more candid and give you more meaningful feedback if their responses to the survey are gathered by a third party as opposed to by you directly. They are likely to feel uncomfortable sharing difficult truths with you if they don't feel their responses will be treated anonymously, especially when completing the survey for the first time. For this reason, the survey should be administered by an outside organization that can: make and keep appropriate commitments about privacy and data security; compile results online (thus avoiding the problem of "will they recognize my handwriting"); and summarize the results of the survey for you effectively.

Use the results and feedback you receive to evaluate the plan, the functions, and the processes and to make any necessary improvements to all aspects of the business. At no time should the results be shared with the company at large; at no time should individual employees be called out for their comments. Remember, this feedback process is meant to make you a better leader by helping you evaluate your own performance and your company's performance.

In one-on-one coaching sessions, you need to protect people

who trust you enough to share, in confidence, what they consider to be the truth. The same principle applies here. If people share information by means of an employee survey, resist any impulse to be defensive or vindictive. Instead, listen for the truth and ask yourself whether what's been shared with you is something that could help you course-correct.

Insight of Excellence

Implemented properly, an effective employee survey will help you detect the undercurrents that may be gathering within your organization before they turn into a tidal wave.

Use a survey that enables the results to be quantified. Use the same survey each time, so results can be compared to prior surveys. Last but certainly not least, bear in mind that expectations are raised when people are asked for their opinions so you should be prepared to act on the most important and relevant results of the survey.

Create your first individual benchmarks with our comprehensive, complimentary online survey tool, which you'll find here: www.sandler.com/free-employee-survey.

Questions to ask yourself as you implement this best practice include:

→ What are the rules in your organization for conducting employee surveys?

→ What is your biggest fear about something that will be uncovered if you do conduct an employee survey?

→ Are you willing and able to act on the results of an employee survey?

→ What are you trying to uncover or gather additional information about, and what specific questions would uncover that information?

Excellence Best Practice: Creating Tracking Reports to Maintain Control of the Business

The Leaders identify a few key outcomes that can be monitored on a regular basis.

Tracking reports keep your business headed in the right direction by identifying "red flags" that require action and attention. It's better to learn about these issues sooner than later. The goal here is to identify a handful of metrics—key performance indicators (KPIs)—that support rapid and accurate decision making. This helps you control performance by making minor adjustments before they become major impediments to accomplishing your vision.

Tracking reports for KPIs are an essential part of the planning process that give leaders of organizations of excellence a steady flow of meaningful, up-to-date information upon which to base decisions. Leaders choose a reasonable number of key measurements to continually monitor, in much the same way a physician would monitor a patient's vital signs or a driver would check speed, engine temperature, fuel levels, and other key indicators of a race car. These key indicators are often referred to as the "dashboard" for a business.

Below is a sample results-oriented dashboard the leader of ABC Engineering uses to monitor the company's overall performance.

KPI Dashboard					
Time Frame	Net Income	Gross Sales	Customer Complaints	Booked Orders	Billable Capacity (%)
YTD	$1,456,234	$9,467,998	28	321	63%
Current Qtr.	$678,324	$4,522,160	12	153	67%

There is no one right list of KPIs that will work for every business. In addition to standard financial measurements and metrics like customer complaints, you may want to consider future indicators like backlog of business, number of leads generated, or requests for quotation. Many businesses also monitor behavioral KPIs, such as "initial phone or in-person meetings set with new decision makers." This makes sense because such behaviors can be controlled and measured and are leading indicators that support the outcomes you want to produce (in this case, closed sales).

Questions to ask yourself as you implement this best practice include:

→ Why have you chosen the metrics that you have been monitoring?

→ What are other metrics that could provide better forecasting?

→ Are you tracking the appropriate indicators for each market segment?

→ Do you use this information to correct course and stay on track?

Excellence Best Practice: Monitoring Board/Advisory Group Performance

Leaders make sure those who are advising them are providing valid and effective advice.

Leaders of organizations of excellence have at least one board or advisory group they use to share and evaluate key priorities, bounce ideas off, and discuss important decisions. These people bring in experience and differing perspectives, often playing devil's advocate in strategic discussions. If you use a board or advisory group to hold you accountable as a business owner/leader—and you should—it is important for you to do a review on each board/advisory group member.

The board/advisory group should consist of independent thinkers whose only interest is to help you grow your organization. The company's attorney, accountants, or others whose input is already being received and paid for should not be members of the board/advisory group. Bear in mind that friends and relatives are not always the best board/advisory group members—they are too likely to lack objectivity.

Leaders must make sure that those who take on the responsibility of advising them provide valid and effective advice. By the

Excellence Process Insight

You must confirm that you have the right board/advisory group, that you are meeting with them regularly, that you are receiving relevant and timely advice from them, and that you are listening to their insights.

same token, leaders must be coachable enough to benefit from the guidance of these advisors.

On a personal note, I was first introduced to Sandler 30 years ago by participating in a peer group called President's Club; business leaders used the group as an informal board of directors. This arrangement helped my business since I got unemotional feedback with no agenda, and it helped me look at business challenges differently. I didn't know it at the time that I joined, but my participation in President's Club would, in time, set me on the path of working with David Sandler as my boss—and, eventually, leading the company he founded.

Questions to ask yourself as you implement this best practice include:

→ Do you have a board/advisory group?
→ How often do you meet with this group?
→ How are members of this group evaluated?
→ Are you getting what you want from the meetings?

→ Is each member contributing?

→ Are these individuals fulfilling the expectations you established for them when you invited them to be members?

→ Is it time to replace any of the members?

→ Is it time to review the term limits of members to determine if a replacement is needed?

22

Passion

assion is the great accelerator, the variable that makes everything else happen.

You have now reached the sixth P, where you support the passion necessary to take your organization to the excellent level. There is a paradox to consider here. Technically, this is the last of the six steps in the Excellence Process; however, completing it means accepting that the process itself never ends.

We often work with leaders who smile wryly when they talk about what they perceive to be their team's shortcomings. These leaders say things like, "I just wish I could clone myself," or "All I need is ten or twelve more people like me." This kind of "joke" or belief system is really a symptom. It's a sign that the real shortcoming lies with the leader. These leaders need to focus not just on supporting and sustaining their own passion, but on mastering the mentoring, coaching, and change management skills that can help them inspire passion in others.

Passion, in the context of organizational excellence, transcends the typical emotions of excitement and enthusiasm. It incorporates a sense of doing and being your best as a way of life that inspires others. This inspiration includes, but is not limited to, making all six P's the way your organization does business—making them the playbook you return to over and over again.

Once you've grasped this sixth P, you understand the importance of doing everything in your power to prevent a feeling of entitlement or complacency from setting in among leaders who may succeed you. You know that leading an organization to and maintaining a level of excellence is a never-ending, repeating process. This process is driven by the way you communicate, both in words and actions. It's an ongoing personal commitment to engage and inspire everyone who works with you by means of your vision, your mission, your plan, and your commitment to continuous improvement. It is the process of all processes!

Passion does not require you to be the best at every task in your organization. That's impossible. Passion does, however, bring out the best in you to enable you to become laser-focused in achieving your vision. It allows you to spend your time planning and adjusting your plans on a regular basis. It drives you to create the optimum structure to build your organization. It leads you to find the right people. It drives you to become as efficient as possible and create processes that are simple for everyone to follow. It demands accountability from everyone in your organization, especially yourself. Without your passion, your organization will never attain the level of excellence you want—nor will it remain there if you fail to inspire passion in others.

Words of Excellence to Live By

"What's money? A man is a success if he gets up in the morning and goes to bed at night and in between does what he wants to do."

—BOB DYLAN

Over the years. I have worked with many entrepreneurs. Some are passionate about what they do every day; they are passionate about getting their company to its highest peak. They treat the business like a person, always trying to make it better. They maintain a constant "excellence dialogue" with clients and customers because they know that feedback from these people is the ultimate gauge of how the organization as a whole and its individual departments are really doing.

Others, however, aren't passionate about the business but about what the payout will do for them. They are waiting for the payday. My view is that the first kind of passion is higher, more rewarding, and more meaningful, than the second. It's the first kind of passion that sustains great businesses. Between the first and the second kind of passion, there is a kind of fall.

You can sometimes see this loss of passion most clearly in family businesses where the second or third generation has taken over. The people who launched the business may have operated from that first kind of passion, the kind that's rooted in a deep commitment to growing the company because doing so was their life's work—the great masterpiece. Yet often the family members who take over the business from that founder take a very different approach. The second or third generations don't bring the same love for what they do to the workplace, and it shows in every aspect of the business. Where the founders were totally, passionately committed to fulfilling the vision, the second or third generation may be simply interested in the business and its day-to-day operations. They may even come to consider the success of the business as something that they have coming—an entitlement.

This doesn't happen to every family business. But it does happen, in my view, to too many of them. Fortunately, there is a vital best practice that leaders of organizations of excellence can follow to establish and maintain passionate, committed leadership as an intrinsic part of the organizational culture, for the leader and for everyone else.

Here is the passion best practice we'll examine in this chapter.

→ Accelerate!

Excellence Best Practice: Accelerate!

Leaders start all over again—and pick up speed.

As the leader of an organization on the road to excellence, you realize that everything you do, every day, should be undertaken with the aim of sharing your organization's vision and accelerating the process of achieving excellence. You set the goal of returning to each of the six P's on the road to excellence with renewed vigor and energy—as a team.

The Ten Commandments of Acceleration for Business Leaders

1. You recognize your own shortcomings and surround yourself with talented individuals who have the needed expertise.

2. You mentor and coach others to create passion in themselves.

3. You create change initiatives that are inclusive, driven by effective two-way communication, and benefit from the feedback of your team.

4. You know that passion is not an event but a contagious state of mind that embraces constant improvement and is constantly on the lookout for blind spots. With this in mind, you maintain an ongoing "excellence dialogue" with clients and customers.

5. Although you know that it is a mistake for you or anyone else in the organization to try to be the best at everything, you never stop increasing/upgrading your qualifications for your changing job.

6. You are always recruiting good employees.

7. You are always growing employees.

8. You are always creating passion in your employees.

9. You take full advantage of highly qualified advisors who can bring your organization the guidance it needs in specific areas.

10. You stay focused on your vision.

Questions to ask yourself as you implement this best practice include:

→ Are you passionate to be the best?

→ Within legal, moral, and ethical boundaries, are you willing and able to do whatever it takes to achieve your vision?

→ Are you willing and able to grow and develop others to be their best?

→ Have you made the Six P's of the Excellence Process the recurring playbook for growing your business?

EPILOGUE

Moving Beyond the Corporate Comfort Zone

> ### Words of Excellence to Live By
>
> ---
>
> "The only person you are destined to become is the person you decide to be."
>
> **—RALPH WALDO EMERSON**

Emerson was absolutely right; the only person you, the leader, are meant to become is the leader you decide to be. Emerson could just as easily have said that the company you are meant to lead is always a function of the person you, the leader, decide to be.

Your own hard work and desire are not enough to ensure that your business will flourish in today's marketplace. You need a process. Unfortunately, people resist process. That's why you must play the lead role in the ongoing road show that is organizational excellence.

If there is to be a culture of passion for continuous growth and improvement in your organization, a culture that moves yourself, your people, and your organization out of the borders of whatever the current comfort zone may be, and into the realm of possibility, it must come from you.

What I have shared with you in this book can be broken down into two deceptively simple-sounding pieces of advice: Keep a constant lookout for the blind spots you've learned about here, and lead your organization moving along the road to excellence by implementing the Six P's on a constant, never-ending basis. I hope you'll keep in touch with me as you make that journey and let me know how it's going for you. My contact information is below.

Let me share one final point. From time to time, you may be tempted to believe that your company's rate of speed along the road to excellence is dependent upon your ability to work on your

Words of Excellence to Live By

"If we can learn to deal with our discomfort and just relax into it, we'll have a better life."

—**MELODY HOBSON,** President of Ariel Investments, Chairwoman of the Board of Dreamworks Animation team. I'm here to tell you that what matters far more is your ability to work on yourself. If you make a habit of always starting there, with the person you see in the mirror, I believe you'll succeed in moving beyond your own comfort zones—and I believe the organization you lead will, by definition, move out of its comfort zone, too. Excellence is a direction, not a destination. As the business landscape evolves and as markets shift, your pursuit of excellence must evolve as well.

I look forward to hearing from you and to sharing the journey. At Sandler, every professional is important to us. If you're willing to share, I want to hear more about your journey to success. Feel free to connect with me on LinkedIn and send me a private message, or you can email me at the address below.

David Mattson
ceo@sandler.com

APPENDIX

Case Study: The Single Best Way to Build an Excellence Organization Is to Avoid Mistakes in the Recruiting and Hiring Process

Three Blind Spots—and How Splunk Avoided Them

Frank Cespedes and David Mattson

I t's common for leaders of sales teams to focus almost exclusively on short-term tactics and current operations while failing to think and act in a way that supports the longer-term needs of their businesses—and it's hard to fault them. Sales teams must meet the immediate needs of their customers, respond issue

Reprinted by permission of Harvard Business Review. *From "How a Fast-Growing Startup Built Its Sales Team for Long-Term Success," by Frank Cespedes and David Mattson, December 2017. ©2017 by Harvard Business Publishing; all rights reserved.*

by issue and account by account, and meet quarterly goals. As one sales manager noted, "In this job, if you don't survive the short term, you don't need to worry about the long term."

The biggest problem with a short-term approach is that managers develop blind spots around crucial processes such as recruiting, hiring, and training and development.

These blind spots are especially prevalent in growing firms where a common rationalization—"I know those issues are important, and I'll get to them when the quarter closes and things settle down"—often shapes management's attention. But ignoring talent processes and strategies can have unintended consequences and stall one's scaling efforts. There are ways to avoid these blind spots, however.

Splunk, a San Francisco-based B2B software firm, is a case in point. Founded in 2003 with $40 million in venture capital funding, Splunk was among the first companies to target the "big data" space. It had no track record to point to when targeting and interacting with top talent during its early years, and indeed no recognized industry to point to. This situation soon necessitated a creative approach to recruiting, hiring, and training. During the critical early years, moreover, there was a big internal debate at Splunk about allocating time and resources to these activities. Many felt that money and time were best devoted to other activities, ranging from R&D to trade shows.

Here are some insights on how Splunk avoided the blind spots as it scaled.

Recruiting

Any business process is only as good as the people involved. Recruiting—an uncertain and expensive process—is no exception, especially in sales where differences in individual performance are stark. The best salespeople generate orders-of-magnitude more than their average peers: from three to ten times more, depending upon the sales context. Talent matters.

"For recruitment," says Bart Fanelli, Splunk's Vice President of Global Field Success, "we set our sights on talent from companies already operating at the level we want to operate at." That's a process which requires leadership time and resources, not just a speech about talent at an off-site. So if you're a $50 million company and your goal is to grow to $250 million, consider targeting hires from firms operating at that level or higher. And to do that, you must make recruitment and hiring an ongoing part of the management culture, not only an HR responsibility.

Interviewing and Hiring

Managers are excessively confident about their ability to evaluate candidates based on personal interviews. Across job categories, there is almost no correlation between interview performance and on-the-job performance. In fact, some studies indicate that interviews can hurt in selection decisions—the firm would have been better off selecting at random! This danger is prevalent in sales. Choosing for an activity where talent varies widely often leads to a cloning bias; many sales managers hire in their own image and assume sole personal control of the interviews.

Better results occur when companies complement a manager's

assessment with multiple interviews with diverse people (to off-set the cloning bias), establish a structured process (so comparisons can be made across common factors), and emphasize behavioral criteria (because gut-feel does not scale). This approach is best supported by simulations, assessments, onboarding programs, and other means that technology is making less costly. But the real constraint remains management's commitment to establishing, communicating, and keeping up-to-date a clear hiring process.

Splunk developed profiles that specified skills and capabilities relevant to each role. They also established certain behavioral elements, which, in management's view, were important across roles. For a field sales position, for example, Splunk specified skills that managers could look for and discuss in the applicant's work history during interviews, e.g., forecast accuracy, messages to relevant market segments, and other categories.

Behavioral elements refer to the on-the-job choices that people make. For instance, is the candidate coachable? Does he or she interact with others without giving a sense of being entitled to special treatment? [Does he or she] work hard without being offensive or disruptive in a negative way with others?

Fanelli notes, "We believe both types of screening criteria—skills [that] are applicable to the specific job and culturally-compatible behaviors that we seek in all of our people—are equally important. We all own the culture and I don't believe that any company can make a habit of hiring brilliant jerks."

As Splunk grew, these profiles were updated, refined, and became the focus of quarterly reviews. After hiring, sales managers were accountable for coaching and developing their people based on the elements specified in the profile. "Our assumption," Fannelli explains, "is that if we understand our business, if we get and keep the profiles right, and if we execute the process consistently, we will succeed. The quarterly reviews help to prevent the common scenario where down the road management is sweeping up broken glass due to performance or interpersonal behaviors."

Processes like this create a healthy mindset. You'll soon realize that there is only a finite universe of great people out there, and that, in order to land them, you'll need to improve upon and fine-tune your approach to interviews and hiring. And, hopefully, you'll learn that great recruitment practices create a multiplier effect—creating a network of good hires generates referrals to more good hires.

Training and Development

Blindness can be a degenerative organizational malady. Many companies, as Fanelli puts it, "reduce their field of vision by following a hire-and-forget approach."

In a given year across industries, over a third of firms do not train salespeople at all, and common practice has training budgets increase when sales are good and decrease when sales are tough. This approach is not only (in a time-honored phrase) bass-ackwards; it also makes it hard to determine cause and effect. Effective sales training, like most useful development, cannot be a single event. People need reinforcement, periodic upgrading, advice on adapting their skills to new circumstances, and motivational help.

A key is to focus training and development on an analysis of current sales tasks and put in place a process that gives [sales representatives], their managers, and leadership timely feedback as they move forward on performance goals.

To scale, you must control what you can control. In Splunk's case, as Fanelli notes, "we kept a certain leader-to-contributor ratio in mind to make sure the first-line sales leader can train contributors on the desired skills. We track this quarterly, looking at training and coaching with the same attention that we use to review 'the numbers' because the effectiveness of our first-line leaders is the gateway to the performance we want to see in sales outcomes."

Any sales force is composed of people with different temperaments, capabilities, and learning styles. To be effective, coaching and development must adapt to the individual and be updated. A regular review cadence in the sales organization drives the process up the chain and makes it an ongoing developmental tool. "The first-line review process," says Fanelli, "connects quarterly to every manager in the field. The second-line review (a review of those who manage and review the first-line managers) focuses on a broader set of skills, happens annually, and goes into more depth than the quarterly process."

Splunk uses a variety of good practices that have helped it avoid common blind spots in sales as it's grown. But our intent is not to suggest that all companies should do what Splunk does. Markets are different, strategies vary, and so specific practices will and should vary. The lesson is that, once you get beyond lip-service about talent, any company must be worthy of talent by making core processes like recruiting, interviewing, and development a real priority in daily practice.

Frank Cespedes *teaches at Harvard Business School and is the author most recently of* Aligning Strategy and Sales *(Harvard Business Review Press).*

David Mattson *is the CEO of Sandler Training, an international training and consulting organization headquartered in the United States.*

Excellence Is a Direction, Not a Destination

Ready to take what you've learned to the next level? Sandler's Leadership for Organizational Excellence training program turns the principles you have discovered in this book into daily operational realities for your firm. It gives your company a detailed, customized roadmap to organizational excellence—and helps you and your team make excellence a way of doing business.

S Sandler Training (with design) is a registered service mark of Sandler Systems, Inc.   Sandler Training

To learn more about this powerful leadership development program from Sandler Training, visit www.Sandler.com/LFOE today.